Plant-based just got better

Big Veg Energy

CHRISTINA SOTERIOU

Interlink Books

an imprint of Interlink Publishing Group, Inc.
Northampton, Massachusetts

Welcome	6
About the Author	8
Get into the Ingredients	10
Ten Money-Saving Tips	11
Vegan Myths Debunked	12

CHAPTER 1
Small Plates 16

CHAPTER 2
Big Platters 60

CHAPTER 3
Cozy Bowls 104

CHAPTER 4
Baking Dish 154

CHAPTER 5
Dessert Spoon 198

Little Jars	232
How to Store Your Fresh Produce	244
Index	248
Acknowledgments	254
Conversion Tables	255

Welcome

Welcome to the long-time vegans. I hope you find here inspiration, ideas and tricks you've never tried before.

Welcome to the active flexitarians. You already know that a plant-forward diet without strict restrictions is amazing for your health and the planet. Every plant-based choice is a positive one.

Welcome to those who never expected to embrace vegan food but have picked up some plant-based habits, despite the odds. Keep up the positive changes and reap the benefits.

Welcome to the omnivores. I hope you find comfort, heartiness and pleasure in these recipes.

Welcome to the next generations, alert and ready to take on the world, one chickpea at a time.

And welcome to anyone in between. This book is for everyone.

About the Author

I grew up in Cyprus, where (until recently) not eating meat was unheard of outside of Lent. I stopped eating meat when I was ten, when I made the connection between a live chicken I had seen and the chicken my mom put on my plate to eat. I didn't eat meat again after that day, mostly because I loved animals so much. I continued to eat fish until I was about fifteen, when I started reading about the ethical, environmental and health issues surrounding animal consumption; of course, fish are a huge part of this. The reasoning behind my choices developed and strengthened, and my decision broadened from being purely emotive to being based on what I had learned.

I had to dig deep to stay firm through decades of arguments with family, friends and doctors who told me to eat "normally." I had gathered a collection of hard truths to dish out to convince others to join me, but I found that, as much as I tried, I couldn't convince anyone else to go vegan with me. That's when I changed my tactics and started feeding everyone instead. Rather than trying to convince people to eat fewer animal products, I cooked for them. Every meal I cooked for my friends and family was one less meal made with animal products, and for me that was—and still is—a huge win.

I got better and better at cooking so that more and more people would enjoy my vegan food and see that eating this way really could be great. I eventually quit my job and started a career in food. I gained an holistic nutrition certification, started a catering business in Cyprus, taught cooking workshops in Chicago, took on private catering and events, worked in recipe development and as a restaurant chef in London, and then I started sharing online. And here we are!

These days, I get to share my food and connect with people I have never met, people in all different places and walks of life, which feels like such a gift. Writing this book for you has been a joy and I really hope that it serves you well.

Get into the Ingredients

You might find a few unfamiliar ingredients in this book, but I promise that they are all worth exploring. Once you become familiar with them, you'll find they have a multitude of uses in various recipes, way beyond the ones in this book. Here are some of my favorites.

MISO

A traditional Japanese fermented paste made from soy beans, rice or barley, salt and a fermentation starter. It adds a savory, umami flavor to soups, dressings and marinades, as well as sweet recipes.

TAHINI/TAHINA

A paste made from ground sesame seeds, rich in healthy fats and protein. It is commonly used in Middle Eastern, Mediterranean and North African cuisines as a key ingredient in hummus, dressings, sauces and even desserts. I haven't come across a supermarket brand worth buying, so I recommend buying tahini that's been produced in the Middle East. Good tahini is light or golden in color, runny and completely smooth.

NUTRITIONAL YEAST

A deactivated yeast that adds a cheesy, nutty flavor to dishes. It is often used as a vegan substitute for cheese, sprinkled on to pastas, or incorporated into sauces and dressings.

AGAVE

A natural sweetener derived from the agave plant, it is often used as an alternative to refined sugar in beverages, baking and desserts. You can always swap this out for maple syrup if you prefer.

HARISSA

A spicy North African chile paste made from roasted peppers, spices and herbs. It adds heat and a depth of flavor to dishes like stews, soups, marinades and spreads.

APPLE CIDER VINEGAR

Made from fermented apple juice, it has a tangy flavor and is used in dressings, marinades and various recipes as a flavor enhancer or for its potential health benefits.

FLAXSEED

Tiny seeds rich in omega-3 fatty acids, fiber and antioxidants. They can be ground and used as an egg substitute (they work as a binding agent), or added to smoothies, cereals or baked goods for added nutrition.

CHICKPEA FLOUR/GRAM FLOUR

A gluten-free flour made from ground chickpeas, it is used in many vegan recipes as a binder or thickener, and can also be used for making chickpea pancakes (socca) or chickpea "tofu," along with endless other uses.

CHILE OIL

Infused oil made by frying chile peppers in oil and aromatics, this adds a spicy kick and flavor to stir-fries, marinades and more. Find it in your local Asian supermarket, online or in large supermarkets. There are many different brands with different spice levels, but my favorite is the iconic Lao Gan Ma brand.

Ten Money-Saving Tips

Adopting a vegan lifestyle doesn't have to be expensive. By being mindful of your choices, planning ahead and making use of affordable, whole-food ingredients, you can enjoy a healthy, budget-friendly vegan diet.

1. **LABEL EVERYTHING**
   Store sauces, marinades, dressings and any leftovers in Tupperware or jars labeled with the contents and the date they were made. This is a tip I learned working in restaurants and it's an easy way to make sure you use up what you have; you are more likely to use it if you know what it is and how soon you need to finish it. Miscellaneous items are often forgotten and ultimately end up in the trash. You just need a roll of masking tape and a marker and you can date and label everything.

2. **PLAN A FRIDGE RAID**
   Designate a day of the week to clear out your fridge and identify any cooked or non-cooked food that needs using up. This will help reduce food waste and your shopping bill.

3. **GO TO INTERNATIONAL SHOPS**
   See if you have any Turkish, Polish, Indian or other international shops close by, as they tend to have cheaper versions of things you might already be buying from the supermarket.

4. **BUY IN BULK**
   Purchase staples like grains, legumes, nuts and seeds in bulk (if you have the space to store them), as they will usually be much cheaper.

5. **TRY BULK-COOKING AND MEAL-PREPPING**
   Cook large batches of meals and freeze individual portions for later use. This not only saves time but also helps you avoid relying on expensive takeout or convenience foods when you're in a hurry. Planning your meals in advance and making a shopping list also helps you avoid impulse purchases.

6. **CHOOSE SEASONAL AND LOCAL PRODUCE**
   Opt for seasonal fruits and vegetables as they tend to be more affordable and flavorful. Visit local farmers' markets or grocery stores if they're close by. See page 244 for tips on keeping produce fresh for longer.

7. **MAKE USE OF FROZEN AND CANNED FOODS**
   Frozen fruits and vegetables can be a budget-friendly alternative to fresh produce, especially when out of season. Canned beans, lentils and tomatoes are also convenient and cost-effective options that you should always have on hand.

8. **GROW YOUR OWN**
   If you have the space and resources, try growing your own herbs, fruits and vegetables. It can save you lots of money in the long run. You can replant store-bought herbs and use old plant-milk cartons as plant pots to cut costs.

9. **REPURPOSE LEFTOVERS**
   Get creative with leftovers and transform them into new dishes. For example, use leftover cooked vegetables in a stir-fry or blend them into a soup. This helps reduce food waste and saves money by maximizing the use of ingredients.

10. **SWAP INGREDIENTS**
    Don't be afraid to substitute ingredients in recipes based on what you have on hand. Although I will suggest specific ingredients in these recipes, I would rather you use up what you have than let anything go to waste. Get creative! Also, if you're transitioning to a vegan lifestyle, use up what you have before buying new vegan alternatives.

Vegan Myths Debunked

MYTH

VEGANS DON'T GET ENOUGH PROTEIN

FACT

Vegans can easily meet their protein needs through a balanced diet that includes a wide variety of plant protein sources, such as legumes (beans, lentils, chickpeas), soy products (tofu, tempeh, edamame), quinoa, nuts and seeds, whole grains and vegetables. Plant proteins may have slightly different amino acid profiles compared to animal proteins, but as long as your diet includes lots of different plant protein sources throughout the day and week, you should hit your protein intake with no problem at all. Protein deficiency is rare in well-nourished people, regardless of their specific dietary choices.

FACT

While some vegan specialty products can be expensive (as non-vegan products can also be), a plant-based diet can easily be affordable. Staples like grains, legumes, fruits, vegetables, nuts and seeds are inexpensive and can form the basis of a nutritious and budget-friendly diet. Avoiding processed vegan convenience foods helps to keep costs down, and I don't use these in my recipes (with the exception of the option to add vegan cheese here and there). I have included tips for saving money on page 11.

MYTH

EATING VEGAN IS EXPENSIVE

MYTH

VEGANS DON'T GET ENOUGH IRON

FACT

There are many plant-based sources of iron, including legumes, dark leafy greens, fortified cereals, quinoa, tofu, tempeh and pumpkin seeds. While iron from plant sources may be less readily absorbed by the body than iron from animal sources, pairing iron-rich foods with vitamin C-rich foods (such as citrus fruits) enhances absorption. That's why you will often see lemon juice as a finishing ingredient in my recipes with dark leafy greens.

FACT

In my view, one of the best things about being vegan is that you can eat more! Plant-based foods, particularly whole plant foods such as fruits, vegetables, legumes and whole grains, tend to be lower in calorie density compared to processed or animal-based foods. This means that you may need to consume larger volumes of food to meet your calorie needs. If you're not consuming enough calories or not choosing calorie-dense plant-based foods, then yes, you may feel hungry.

On the flip side, plant-based diets tend to be higher in fiber, which can promote feelings of fullness. If you're not used to a high-fiber diet, it can take some time for your body to adjust. Initially, you might experience increased bowel movements or a feeling of fullness or bloating, but this typically subsides as your digestive system adapts. Give your body time to adjust and introduce new foods slowly.

MYTH

A VEGAN DIET WILL LEAVE YOU FEELING HUNGRY

MYTH

B12 DEFICIENCY IS A VEGAN ISSUE

FACT

Vitamin B12 is primarily found in animal-derived products; however, B12 deficiency is not exclusive to vegans. Many non-vegans also experience deficiencies due to factors including poor dietary choices, age or gastrointestinal issues.

It's important to note that while animal products are sources of B12, the animals themselves do not produce the vitamin at all. Instead, certain bacteria, fungi and archaea in the environment, including soil and water, are responsible for synthesizing B12. Animals obtain B12 by consuming foods contaminated with these B12-producing microorganisms, or by being given B12 supplements, which is usually the case in modern animal farming. You can take B12 supplements yourself to get the vitamin directly rather than getting it indirectly through products from animals that have been fed or injected with B12.

Vitamin B12 plays a crucial role in various bodily processes, so it's important for everyone to regularly take B12 supplements if not eating animal products.

FACT

Calcium can be obtained from plant-based sources such as fortified plant-based milk, tofu, tempeh, leafy greens (kale, collards, broccoli), sesame and chia seeds, almonds and fortified orange juice. Vegans can easily meet their calcium needs through a well-rounded plant-based diet.

MYTH

CALCIUM IS ONLY AVAILABLE FROM MILK

MYTH

VEGANS CANNOT BE ATHLETIC OR STRONG

FACT

Many successful athletes follow a vegan diet and excel in their sports. Plant-based foods can definitely provide the carbohydrates, proteins and fats necessary for peak athletic performance, as long as they are balanced and plentiful. Boxer David Haye, tennis players Venus and Serena Williams, strongman Patrik Baboumian, UFC fighter Nate Diaz and racing driver Lewis Hamilton are all inspiring examples of vegan athletes.

MYTH

EATING VEGAN IS BAD FOR THE ENVIRONMENT

FACT

Plant-based diets have been shown to have a much lower environmental impact compared to diets heavy in animal products. Animal agriculture is resource-intensive and contributes to deforestation, greenhouse gas emissions and water pollution. By choosing plant-based options, individuals can reduce their carbon footprints and contribute to a more sustainable food system.

MYTH

SOY PRODUCTS ARE UNHEALTHY AND AFFECT YOUR HORMONES

FACT

There is a misconception that tofu contains high levels of hormones, specifically oestrogen. However, tofu does not naturally contain hormones. Soy beans, the main ingredient in tofu, do contain phytoestrogens, which are plant-based compounds that can mimic weak oestrogen activity in the body. Phytoestrogens have been studied for their potential health benefits, and moderate consumption of soy products like tofu is safe and beneficial for most people. Tofu is nutrient-rich, high in protein, rich in minerals and low in saturated fats, and also contains zero cholesterol (unlike high-protein animal products). I hope my tofu recipes in this book inspire you to try different types in different ways.

Small
Plates

Many cultures have their own version of small plates: in Spain there is tapas, in Greece and Cyprus we have our mezze, and countries all over the Middle East have their own mezza or mezze. The idea is the same: a selection of small plates served and shared as a meal. While lots of the plates in this chapter were developed with sharing in mind, they are also perfect as standalone dishes, appetizers or snacks. My favorite thing about food, which I learned from my mom, is that it's much more special when it's shared.

Pulled Leeks with Pistachio Cream

This is my favorite way to eat leeks—cooked on a flame or in the oven until charred on the outside and perfectly caramelized on the inside, then pulled into long, thick ribbons. It gives them a wonderful texture that goes so well with the roasted pistachio cream. Serve as a side, a dip, on toast or even swirled through tagliatelle.

SERVES 2-4
1 hour 45 minutes

INGREDIENTS

4	Leeks
¾ CUP (100 G)	Pistachios
7 OZ (200 G)	Vegan cream cheese (gluten-free if needed)
–	Juice of 1 lemon
–	Salt, freshly ground black pepper and olive oil

1. Preheat the oven to 425°F (220°C).

2. Trim the toughest green edges off the leeks, then wash the leeks by holding the top side under running water to flood them, before quickly turning them over to drain. This should flush out any dirt.

3. If you have a gas stove, you can maximize the flavor by burning the leeks over an open flame before roasting them. Use metal tongs to hold the leeks over the flame and turn to scorch all over, working with care. If you are lucky enough to have a grill, you could use this to char the leeks before continuing with the next step.

4. Transfer the leeks to a roasting pan and roast in the oven for 1–1½ hours, turning once, until black and crispy all over.

5. Meanwhile, tip the pistachios onto a baking sheet and toast in the oven for about 5 minutes until golden, tossing once. Set aside a small handful for garnish, then transfer the rest into a small food processor. Process until you have a crumb or a paste. Add the vegan cream cheese and a good squeeze of lemon and blend again until smooth. Season to taste with salt and pepper, and more lemon if you like. Set aside.

6. When the leeks have finished roasting, allow to cool before peeling off and discarding the blackened outer layers. Now gently pull the leeks apart, shredding them into long strips. Tip these into a bowl and season with salt and pepper. Add a tiny drizzle of olive oil, then gently toss with your hands.

7. Roughly chop the reserved pistachios.

8. To serve, spoon the pistachio cream into a small bowl and top with the leeks and chopped pistachios. Finish with a final squeeze of lemon.

● GLUTEN-FREE

Miso Quinoa Beet Burgers

I used to make these burgers for events and sell them in the little kitchen that I rented in Cyprus. They have a perfect burger texture and are so full of flavor, you would never guess how nutrient dense they actually are. They are great for meal prep as they freeze really well, so make a big batch and keep some in the freezer to add to salads, wraps or roasted veggies.

MAKES 12 SMALL PATTIES OR 6 BIG ONES

1 hour

INGREDIENTS

⅓ CUP (70 G)	Quinoa
1 LB (450 G)	Raw beets (4–5 medium beets)
½ OZ (15 G)	Sun-dried tomatoes
1	Red onion
3	Garlic cloves
1½ TBSP	Miso paste
¾–1 CUP (90 G)	Buckwheat flour or chickpea flour
2 TBSP	Dijon mustard
2 TBSP	Ground flaxseed
1 TBSP	Sesame seeds (optional, for topping)
—	Salt, freshly ground black pepper and olive oil

TIPS

TO COOK THESE IN AN AIR FRYER, COOK AT 400°F (200°C) FOR 5 MINUTES, THEN FLIP AND COOK FOR ANOTHER 2 MINUTES.

THESE PATTIES CAN BE FROZEN BEFORE COOKING, SO ARE GREAT TO MAKE IN BIG BATCHES. SIMPLY MAKE THE MIXTURE AND SHAPE THE PATTIES, THEN LAY THEM FLAT ON A TRAY IN THE FREEZER. ONCE FROZEN, STACK THEM IN A CONTAINER OR A FREEZER BAG WITH A SHEET OF PARCHMENT PAPER BETWEEN LAYERS SO THEY DON'T STICK TOGETHER. YOU CAN COOK THEM FROM FROZEN; JUST ADD ANOTHER 10 MINUTES TO THE COOKING TIME.

1. Preheat the oven to 425°F (220°C) and line a baking sheet with parchment paper.

2. Rinse the quinoa and put it into a saucepan with plenty of water. Bring to a boil, then reduce the heat to a simmer and cook for 15 minutes. Drain, then tip the cooked quinoa on to a large tray. Spread it out and leave to cool.

3. Meanwhile, peel and roughly chop the beets, and roughly chop the sun-dried tomatoes, onion and garlic. Add all of these to a food processor, along with the cooled quinoa, and process until you have a rough paste with pieces no bigger than grains of couscous. If you don't have a food processor, you can mince the garlic, finely chop the onion and grate the beets, then mix it all together well.

4. Pour the mixture into a large frying pan and season well. Sauté for 6–8 minutes over medium heat until fragrant and most of the moisture has evaporated.

5. If your pan is big enough, you can save on some dish-washing by adding the rest of the ingredients (except the oil) to the pan and mixing well (do this off the heat). Otherwise, dump everything into a bowl and mix well. If using a bowl, it's best to use your hands here to really bring everything together; the beets won't stain as much when they're cooked.

6. Shape the mixture into evenly sized patties, either 6 big burger-sized ones or 12 smaller ones. Lay them on the prepared baking sheet and brush with a little oil. Bake in the oven for 12 minutes, then flip, brush with a little more oil if you like, and bake for another 12 minutes. Serve sprinkled with sesame seeds, if you like.

● GLUTEN-FREE ● NUT-FREE

Warm Dates with Pistachios & Preserved Lemon

These gooey, warm dates are possibly the most delicious thing you can make in 5 minutes. Enjoy as a snack or as part of a mezze, with a dollop of soy yogurt. You could also smoosh them onto some crusty bread, chop them up and add to a crisp salad, or throw them into pasta or roasted veggies.

SERVES 4–8
15 minutes

INGREDIENTS

- 1 Small preserved lemon (optional)
- — Handful of pistachios
- 10 Medjool dates
- — Zest of 1 lemon
- — Flaky sea salt and olive oil

TO SERVE (OPTIONAL)

- — Plain vegan yogurt (gluten-free if needed)
- — Toasted crusty bread (gluten-free if needed)

1. Finely slice and deseed the preserved lemon, if using.

2. Lightly toast the pistachios in a hot, dry pan for 3–5 minutes over low-medium heat, until golden and fragrant.

3. Add just enough olive oil to coat the bottom of a small frying pan or saucepan and place over low-medium heat. Add the dates and heat gently for about 5 minutes until soft and warmed through. At the very end, add the preserved lemon slices, if using. Take care not to overcook as they will disintegrate.

4. To serve, spoon the dates and lemon onto a small plate and drizzle over some olive oil. Sprinkle over the pistachios, lemon zest and a little flaky sea salt. If you like, add a dollop of yogurt on the side and enjoy with some toasted crusty bread. Take care when eating—make sure you remove the date pits first. These are best served warm, immediately after cooking.

● GLUTEN-FREE   ● ALLIUM-FREE

Artichoke, Spinach & Cheese Pastry Pockets

This deliciously simple pastry is inspired by Turkish gozleme. I've swapped the traditional unleavened dough for filo pastry to make it quicker and easier, but it's just as tasty. This is great served with a salad for a quick lunch or brunch, but you can also serve it as an appetizer or as part of a spread.

SERVES 4
35 minutes

INGREDIENTS

2–3	Garlic cloves
1 TBSP	Olive oil, plus extra for brushing
7 OZ (200 G)	Baby spinach
14 OZ (400 G)	Can of butter beans
1½ TBSP	Vegan pesto
5½ OZ (160 G)	Jarred marinated artichokes
—	Juice of ½ lemon
2 LARGE (OR 4 SMALL)	Filo pastry sheets (most brands are vegan but check the ingredients)
1½ CUPS (160 G)	Grated vegan cheese
—	Salt and freshly ground black pepper

1. Mince or finely chop the garlic cloves.

2. Heat the olive oil in a large frying pan over medium heat. Add the garlic and spinach, season with salt and pepper, and sauté until the spinach has wilted. Remove from the pan and set aside in a bowl.

3. Drain the beans and add them to a second large bowl. Add the pesto. Using a fork or a potato masher, crush the beans until they are very soft and the pesto is mixed through.

4. Drain the artichokes and finely chop them. Add them to the bowl of butter bean mash, along with the cooked spinach, and stir well to combine. Squeeze in the lemon juice and season to taste with salt and lots of pepper.

5. Cut the two large sheets of filo in half, so you have four pieces. Add a quarter of the butter bean mixture to the middle of one of the cut sheets, and top with a quarter of the vegan cheese. Fold up the sides on the two longest edges about ¾ in (2 cm) in. Then fold up the two other sides, overlapping them slightly. Brush the undersides with a little oil to help stick. You should have a neat little parcel. Repeat with the remaining pastry sheets and filling.

6. Brush the pastry parcels on one side with a little olive oil. Heat a dry frying pan over medium heat. Add two of the pockets and cook for about 1 minute 30 seconds on each side until brown and crispy. Transfer to a plate and repeat with the remaining pockets.

7. Slice the pastry pockets in half to serve. These are best enjoyed fresh, but will keep in the fridge for a day or two. Reheat any leftovers in a hot, dry pan.

Blistered Green Beans with Ginger Tomatoes

This recipe is a marriage of two dishes, from different sides of the world, using the same ingredient: the humble green bean. One is a Cypriot dish called fasolakia yiahni, which is tomatoey, garlicky, homey and delicious, and the other is a Chinese dish of flash-fried green beans with lots of garlic. Serve as a side or pile onto fluffy jasmine rice.

SERVES 2–4
15 minutes

INGREDIENTS

10½ OZ (300 G)	Green beans
1½ TBSP	Sunflower oil or canola oil
3	Medium-sized tomatoes (not too ripe)
1½ TBSP (20 G)	Fresh root ginger
2	Garlic cloves
2 TSP	Dark soy sauce (or tamari if gluten-free)
1 TSP	Sesame oil
⅓ CUP (30 G)	Sliced almonds
1–2 TSP	Chile flakes
—	Salt and freshly ground black pepper

1. Trim the green beans. Heat the oil in a large frying pan over medium-high heat. Add the green beans and a pinch of salt to the pan and fry for 8–10 minutes, tossing occasionally, until soft and charred in spots.

2. While the beans are cooking, make the tomato sauce. Grate the tomatoes into a bowl, then chop up any remaining tomato skin and add this to the bowl too. Finely grate the ginger (no need to peel it, just give it a good scrub) into the bowl, along with the garlic. Add the soy sauce and sesame oil and a good pinch of salt and pepper, and stir to combine.

3. Meanwhile, lightly toast the sliced almonds in a dry frying pan over medium-low heat for 2–3 minutes until golden and fragrant. Stir often and take care not to let them burn.

4. When the beans are ready, add the tomato mixture to the pan and reduce the heat to low. Toss to combine and cook for about 2 minutes until the garlic is fragrant and the tomatoes have thickened slightly into a sauce, stirring often. Add a splash of water if it thickens too much. Taste and adjust the seasoning, adding a little more soy sauce for saltiness, if you like.

5. To serve, tip the tomato and bean mixture onto a large plate and sprinkle over the almonds and chile flakes.

Broccoli Stems & Charred Broccoli Snow

This recipe utilizes broccoli in two ways: the stems are roasted until caramelized but with a firm bite, and most of the florets are grated and charred with garlic to create a really appealing "snow"-like texture. It all sits on a creamy, Japanese-inspired sauce that's an unassuming flavor-bomb. It looks impressive but it's really simple to make. Serve as an appetizer or with steamed rice and edamame for a full meal.

SERVES 2
40 minutes

INGREDIENTS

2	Medium-sized broccoli heads
2 TBSP	Olive oil, plus extra for drizzling
2–3	Garlic cloves
2 TBSP	Crispy chile oil (check the label if it needs to be nut-free)
2 TBSP	White sesame seeds
—	Salt and freshly ground black pepper

FOR THE GOMA DARE SAUCE

¼ CUP (60 G)	Tahini
¼ CUP (60 G)	Vegan mayonnaise
2 TBSP	Rice vinegar
4 TSP	Light soy sauce
1 TSP	Miso paste
2 TSP	Maple syrup

1. Preheat the oven to 425°F (220°C).

2. Place the first head of broccoli upside down on a chopping board with the stem pointing upwards. Carefully slice off the florets, working from the outside inwards, with the knife pointing down, until you are left with just the stem with some florets attached. Slice the stem lengthways into quarters so you have four long stems with a few florets at the top. Repeat with the other broccoli head. Drizzle with a little olive oil and season with salt and pepper.

3. Place the broccoli stem pieces on a baking sheet and roast for 15–18 minutes until they start to char. Pierce them with a sharp knife to check they are done; they should be soft inside and crispy outside.

4. Meanwhile, coarsely grate the removed broccoli florets. Use a knife to finely chop the ends that you can't grate. Tip into a large bowl. Finely mince the garlic and use your fingers to crumble it into the grated broccoli. Season well with salt and pepper.

5. Heat the 2 tablespoons of olive oil in a large frying pan over medium heat. Add the grated broccoli mixture and fry for 5–8 minutes, stirring often, until the mixture is mostly crispy and charred with some bright greens left.

6. Meanwhile, make the goma dare sauce. Whisk together the tahini, mayonnaise, rice vinegar, soy sauce, miso and maple syrup. Taste and adjust to your liking.

7. To plate, drizzle most of the goma dare onto a large serving plate, then layer over the roasted broccoli stems. Sprinkle the charred broccoli snow over the top, then finish with dollops of crispy chile oil and a scattering of sesame seeds. Serve.

NUT-FREE

Mushroom Dumplings

Almost every corner of the world has their own version of a dumpling. These are inspired by Turkish manti, but use wonton wrappers to save you time and effort to focus on the filling. Manti are traditionally served with yogurt and a chile sauce, which is what we have here too. These dumplings are delicious, filling and really fun to make, especially if you have guests to impress.

MAKES 16/SERVES 4 AS A SIDE
1 hour

INGREDIENTS

10½ OZ (300 G)	Button mushrooms
1	Small shallot
2	Garlic cloves
1½ OZ (40 G)	Sun-dried tomatoes, plus 2 tbsp of their oil
10 SPRIGS	Flat-leaf parsley
¼ CUP (35 G)	Pine nuts (or swap for chopped walnuts)
1 TSP	Balsamic vinegar
1–3 TSP	Harissa paste (depending on your preference for heat)
2½ OZ (70 G)	Extra-firm tofu
16	Square dumpling wrappers (most brands are vegan, but check the package)
—	Salt and freshly ground black pepper

TO SERVE

1 CUP (250 G)	Plain vegan yogurt
—	Zest and juice of 1 lemon
3 TBSP	Olive oil
¼ TSP	Chile flakes (optional)

1. Finely chop the mushrooms and shallot. Mince the garlic. Chop the sun-dried tomatoes. Finely chop the parsley and set some aside for garnish.

2. Heat the sun-dried tomato oil in a large frying pan over medium heat. Add the shallot and garlic and season with salt and pepper, then sauté for 3–4 minutes until translucent.

3. Add the mushrooms to the pan and sauté for 15–20 minutes until all the liquid has evaporated from the pan and the mushrooms are starting to caramelize. If your pan is on the smaller side, you may need to add half the mushrooms and cook them down before adding the rest.

4. Meanwhile, lightly toast the pine nuts in a dry pan over low heat for 3–5 minutes, until golden. Stir constantly as they can burn very quickly.

5. Tip half the toasted pine nuts into the pan of mushrooms, reserving the rest for later. Now add the balsamic vinegar to the pan, along with the sun-dried tomatoes and three-quarters of the harissa. Crumble in the tofu, then cook for another 5 minutes, stirring often to combine the flavors and allow the balsamic to evaporate.

6. Turn off the heat and stir through the parsley. Taste for seasoning and allow to cool completely before moving on to the next step.

CONTINUED OVERLEAF

RECIPE CONTINUED

7. Fill a small bowl or cup with some water and keep it close by. Lay out one dumpling wrapper and place a heaped teaspoon of filling into the center. Dip a finger into the water and lightly wet all four edges of the wrapper. Bring two opposite corners into the center and pinch to close. Then take the remaining opposite corners and bring those into the center too. Now all four corners should be pinched together in the center. Make sure that the edges are fully closed; the water should make them stick together.

8. Repeat with the remaining filling and wrappers. Cover the finished dumplings with a tea towel to stop them drying out.

9. If you have a steamer basket, line the base of the basket with some parchment paper and set it over a pan of boiling water. Place the dumplings in the basket, making sure they aren't touching each other, otherwise they will stick together. Steam for 5–7 minutes until the wrappers are soft and cooked through.

10. If you don't have a steamer basket, you can lightly poach the dumplings in a wide saucepan with a lid. Pour water into your saucepan to a depth of ½ in (1 cm) and bring to a rolling simmer. Gently add as many dumplings as you can fit in the pan without touching each other and cook, covered, for 4–5 minutes. Repeat until all the dumplings are cooked.

11. Pour the yogurt into a small bowl and stir in the lemon juice and a sprinkle of salt.

12. In another bowl, combine the olive oil with the remaining harissa.

13. To serve, generously spoon the yogurt onto a large plate and sit the dumplings on top. Pour over the harissa oil and then sprinkle with the reserved pine nuts. Finish with plenty of lemon zest and some chile flakes, if you like.

Panisse-Style Chickpea Tofu with Hot Maple Syrup

This is one of two recipes that use chickpea flour to make chickpea tofu, and it really shows how versatile chickpeas can be. This recipe is inspired by French panisse, grilled and drizzled with a spicy maple syrup. It makes a delicious side or appetizer, or as part of a mezze. Serve warm or at room temperature.

SERVES 2–4
20 minutes, plus 1 hour to set

INGREDIENTS

FOR THE CHICKPEA TOFU

1⅔ CUPS (140 G)	Chickpea flour
½ TSP	Salt
—	Sunflower oil or canola oil

FOR THE HOT MAPLE SYRUP

1	Hot red chile
⅓ CUP (80 ML)	Maple syrup
¼ TSP	Smoked paprika (optional, for a smoky flavor)

TO SERVE

1 TBSP	Sesame seeds
1	Small red chile, sliced
5–6	Mint leaves
—	Salt and freshly ground black pepper

TIP

TRY THIS "TOFU" RECIPE IN PLACE OF STORE-BOUGHT TOFU FOR A HOMEMADE ALTERNATIVE. IF YOU LIKE, YOU CAN EXPERIMENT BY ADDING DIFFERENT FLAVORS TO THE BATTER—TRY ADDING TURMERIC, NUTRITIONAL YEAST, CURRY SPICES OR GARLIC AND ONION POWDER IN SMALL AMOUNTS.

1. First, make the chickpea tofu. Find a container measuring around 5 × 8 in (12 × 20 cm). You'll also need a whisk and a spatula.

2. Sift the chickpea flour into a mixing bowl to remove any clumps. Add the salt and stir. Pour in 1¼ cups (300 ml) water, adding it a little at a time and stirring between each addition. This will help avoid clumping. Leave to sit for 5 minutes.

3. Bring another 1¼ cups (300 ml) water to a boil in a saucepan. Once the water is boiling, reduce the heat to low and slowly pour the chickpea mixture into the pan, whisking constantly until it is fully combined and you are sure there are no lumps. Now swap the whisk for a spatula (to avoid bubbles), and continue to stir.

4. After 4–6 minutes, it should start to thicken and have a glossy texture. When this happens, immediately pour the mixture into the container and cover with a piece of parchment paper or plastic wrap directly on the mixture to stop a skin forming. Allow to cool for 15 minutes and transfer to the fridge for 1 hour to set.

5. To make the hot maple syrup, thinly slice the chile and remove the seeds if you like less spice. Pour the maple syrup, chile and smoked paprika (if using) into a small saucepan over low heat and simmer for 5–8 minutes. Strain, or leave the chile slices in the syrup (the heat will continue to develop if you do this).

6. When the chickpea tofu is set, slice into ½ in (1 cm) thick slices. Heat a drizzle of oil in a griddle pan or a non-stick frying pan over high heat. Add the chickpea tofu slices to the pan and fry for 1½–2 minutes until charred and crispy, then flip to char on the other side. Be careful, as they break easily when warm.

7. Transfer the chickpea tofu to a serving plate and season each slice well with salt and pepper. Arrange the pieces so they overlap, then pour over the hot maple syrup. Sprinkle with sesame seeds and fresh chile, then tear over the mint leaves.

● GLUTEN-FREE   ● NUT-FREE   ● ALLIUM-FREE

Chickpea Tofu Salad with Ginger-Soy Dressing

Another recipe using my chickpea tofu, this recipe is inspired by Burmese tofu, with a punchy sauce to match. This salad is even better the next day once the "tofu" has had time to marinate.

SERVES 2–4

15 minutes, plus 1 hour to set

INGREDIENTS

⅔ CUP (100 G)	Cherry tomatoes
1	Small red chile (optional)
—	Handful of Thai basil leaves (or regular basil leaves)

FOR THE CHICKPEA TOFU

1⅔ CUPS (140 G)	Chickpea flour
½ TSP	Salt

FOR THE DRESSING

3 TBSP (40 G)	Fresh root ginger
6	Garlic cloves
3	Scallions
2 TBSP	Neutral oil
4 TBSP	Light soy sauce
2 TBSP	Rice vinegar
1½ TBSP	Soft light brown sugar
½ TSP	Chile flakes
2 TBSP	Sesame seeds (black, white or both), plus extra to serve

1. Begin by making the chickpea tofu. Before you start, find a container measuring around 5 × 8 in (12 × 20 cm) and keep it close by. You'll also need a whisk and a spatula.

2. Sift the chickpea flour into a mixing bowl through a fine sieve to remove any clumps. Add the salt and stir. Pour in 1¼ cups (300 ml) water, adding it a little at a time and stirring between each addition. This will help avoid clumping. Leave to sit for 5 minutes.

3. Bring another 1¼ cups (300 ml) water to a boil in a saucepan over high heat. Once the water is boiling, reduce the heat to low and slowly pour the chickpea mixture into the pan, whisking constantly until it is fully combined and you are sure there are no lumps. Now swap the whisk for a spatula (to avoid bubbles), and continue to stir.

4. After 4–6 minutes, it should start to thicken and take on a glossy texture. When this happens, immediately pour the mixture into the container and cover with a piece of parchment paper or plastic wrap, placing this directly on top of the mixture to stop a skin from forming. Allow to cool for 15 minutes, then transfer to the fridge for at least 1 hour to set.

5. To make the dressing, grate the ginger, mince the garlic and finely slice the scallions, setting aside a handful of the green tops for garnish. Combine the ginger, garlic and scallions in a small bowl with the rest of the dressing ingredients. Taste and adjust the seasoning to your liking.

6. Roughly chop the tomatoes into uneven pieces and slice or cube the chickpea tofu. Finely slice the red chile, if using.

7. To assemble, tip the tomatoes and chickpea tofu into a shallow bowl. Pour over the dressing and tear the basil over the top. Finish with the reserved scallion greens and sliced chile, if using, then scatter over some more sesame seeds and serve.

● NUT-FREE

Zucchini Fritters

In Cyprus, we have a takeout restaurant on almost every corner called a psistaria that serves a range of traditional homemade dishes. My favorites are the zucchini fritters and this is my version of that much-loved dish.

MAKES 12–15 FRITTERS
35 minutes

INGREDIENTS

4	Medium-sized zucchinis (about 1 lb 12 oz/800 g)
1½ TSP	Salt
4	Scallions
2 TBSP (10 G)	Mint leaves
⅓ CUP (20 G)	Flat-leaf parsley
¾ CUP (10 G)	Dill
2	Large garlic cloves
6 TBSP	Nutritional yeast
4 TBSP	Ground flaxseed
1 TSP	Ground cumin
3 TSP	Sesame seeds
—	Zest and juice of 1 lemon
1 TSP	Freshly ground black pepper
¾ CUP (70 G)	Chickpea flour
—	Sunflower oil, for shallow-frying

FOR THE MINTY YOGURT (OPTIONAL)

5–7	Mint leaves
½ CUP (100 G)	Vegan Greek yogurt (gluten-free and nut-free if needed)
—	Olive oil and salt

1. Slice off and discard the tips of the zucchinis and coarsely grate. Tip the grated zucchinis into a colander. Sprinkle with 1 teaspoon of the salt, then place the colander over a bowl and leave to drain for at least 10 minutes. Once this is done, squeeze any remaining water out of the zucchini with your hands and transfer into a large clean bowl.

2. Finely slice the scallions and herbs, and mince the garlic. Add these to the bowl with the grated zucchini, along with the nutritional yeast, flaxseed, ground cumin, sesame seeds, lemon zest and juice, black pepper and the remaining ½ teaspoon salt, then stir. Add the chickpea flour and knead with your hands until the mixture comes together in a sticky dough.

3. Take about 2 tablespoons of the mixture and roll it into an elongated ball in the palm of your hand. Repeat with the remaining mixture; it should yield about 12 fritters.

4. Pour sunflower oil into a non-stick frying pan to a depth of about ¾ in (2 cm). Heat over medium heat. To check that it's hot enough, drop in a tiny amount of batter; if it sizzles immediately, the oil is ready. Add a few fritters to the pan and fry for about 45 seconds on each side, carefully turning them so they become golden brown all over.

5. Transfer to a plate lined with paper towels to soak up any excess oil. Repeat with the remaining fritters, topping up the oil if needed.

6. If you're making the minty yogurt, chop or tear the mint leaves, then combine the yogurt and mint in a small bowl. Drizzle with a little olive oil and a sprinkle of salt, if you like. Serve alongside the fritters.

7. These fritters will keep in the fridge for 3 days and are great both cold and hot. To reheat, put them into a hot oven for 5 minutes to warm through.

● GLUTEN-FREE   ● NUT-FREE

Crispy Artichokes with Nori Mayo

Everything in this recipe will remind you of having lunch by the sea: the nori in the mayo, the briny, crispy artichokes, the lemon squeezed over it all. It's such a simple recipe, but one of my favorites in the book. This makes a nice side or appetizer for Greek or Italian dishes, or you can serve it as part of a mezze.

SERVES 2
25 minutes

INGREDIENTS

2 × 10 OZ (280 G)	Jars of marinated artichokes
1	Large lemon
1	Nori sheet
⅓ CUP (75 G)	Vegan mayonnaise
—	Handful of flat-leaf parsley (optional, for garnish)

1. Preheat the oven to 470°F (240°C).

2. Drain the artichokes and cut them into bite-sized pieces (if they aren't already). Slice half of the lemon into thin rounds.

3. Arrange the artichoke pieces on a baking sheet with plenty of space between them. Roast for 10 minutes, then remove from the oven and flip them over. Add the lemon slices to the baking sheet, placing them in between and on top of the artichokes. Return to the oven for another 10–12 minutes until crispy.

4. Meanwhile, make the nori mayo. Pulse the nori sheet into small pieces (or tear it with your hands) and add it to a small bowl. Add the mayonnaise and squeeze in most of the other half of the lemon, saving a little squeeze for the end. Stir to combine.

5. Tip the roasted artichokes and lemon slices onto a platter. Finish with a squeeze of lemon juice and scatter some parsley leaves over the top, if you like, then serve with the mayo.

● GLUTEN-FREE   ● NUT-FREE

Fridge-Raid Crispy Pancakes

These Korean-inspired pancakes are made with a simple batter and are a great way to use up odds and ends of different veggies like cabbage and carrots. Gochujang is a Korean fermented chile sauce and is really delicious, so give it a try if you haven't yet. You can find it online or in your local Asian supermarket and it keeps for a long time in the fridge. I've suggested some herbs and vegetables that would be tasty in these, but use whatever you have available to save things from going to waste.

SERVES 4
30 minutes

INGREDIENTS

2⅓ CUPS (200 G)	Chickpea flour
2	Garlic cloves
1 TBSP	Light soy sauce
1 TSP	Baking powder
2 TSP	Miso paste (optional)
1	Carrot
10½ OZ (300 G)	Purple or white cabbage
¾–1 OZ (20–30 G)	Mixed herbs such as parsley, basil, cilantro or dill
6–8	Scallions
¾ CUP (100 G)	Corn or frozen peas (thawed)
3 TBSP	Sesame seeds
–	Salt, freshly ground black pepper and neutral oil

FOR THE GOCHUJANG DIPPING SAUCE

3 TBSP	Gochujang paste
1½ TBSP	Agave
1½ TBSP	Sesame oil
3 TBSP	Rice vinegar

1. Combine the chickpea flour, garlic cloves, soy sauce, baking powder and miso, if using, in a blender. Add 1¼ cups (300 ml) water and blend until smooth. Set aside.

2. Grate the carrot (no need to peel it), slice the cabbage very thinly, and roughly chop the herbs. Halve the scallions lengthways, then cut each half into 2 in (5 cm) pieces. Combine all the vegetables, plus the corn or peas, in a large bowl. Pour over the batter and season with salt and pepper. Mix well to fully combine.

3. Heat a drizzle of oil in a large non-stick frying pan over medium-high heat. Use a ladle to spoon some of the batter into the pan, then use a rubber spatula to squash it down slightly on the top and shape it into a round pancake roughly the size of your fist and about ½ in (1 cm) thick. If you have a large frying pan, you should be able to cook three pancakes at a time. Sprinkle some of the sesame seeds over the top of each pancake and cook for 2–2½ minutes until golden, then carefully flip and cook for another 2 minutes on the other side until crispy. Transfer to a plate and cover with foil to keep warm, then repeat with the remaining batter, adding more oil as needed. You should make about 8 pancakes.

4. To make the gochujang dipping sauce, whisk all the ingredients together in a small bowl.

5. Serve the pancakes with the dipping sauce.

Lemony Sunflower Seed Dip

Labneh is a thick, tangy, strained yogurt, usually served as a dip or a base for many Levantine dishes. I've made a close iteration of it here by using sunflower seeds to thicken vegan yogurt, with lots of lemon and nutritional yeast for flavor.

SERVES 2
30 minutes

INGREDIENTS

1½ CUPS (200 G)	Sunflower seeds, plus extra to serve
1 CUP (200 G)	Plain vegan yogurt (gluten-free and nut-free if needed)
⅓ CUP (80 ML)	Lemon juice
1 TSP	Olive oil
4 TSP	Nutritional yeast
1 TSP	Flaky sea salt

FOR THE TOPPINGS

—	Olive oil
—	Pinch of sumac or paprika
1 TBSP	Sunflower seeds
1 TBSP	Finely chopped mint leaves

1. Tip the sunflower seeds into a bowl and pour over enough boiling water to cover. Leave to soak for at least 25 minutes (soak for at least 2 hours or overnight if your blender is not a high-speed one).

2. Drain the soaked sunflower seeds and add them to a blender, along with the yogurt, lemon juice, olive oil, nutritional yeast and salt. Blend until smooth. You may have to keep scraping down the sides of the blender to make sure everything is combined. Add a little more yogurt if your blender still can't get it smooth.

3. Taste and season again if needed, adding more lemon or nutritional yeast according to your preference.

4. To serve, spread the dip over a shallow bowl or plate and pour over a generous drizzle of olive oil. Top with a sprinkle of sumac or paprika, followed by the sunflower seeds and mint.

5. This will keep for 3–4 days in a sealed container in the fridge.

GLUTEN-FREE · NUT-FREE · ALLIUM-FREE

Mini Sesame Toasts

These crispy, crunchy taco-shaped appetizers are a great party dish, one that might make you nostalgic for a Chinese restaurant classic.

MAKES 8
45 minutes

INGREDIENTS

1	Nori sheet
1½ TBSP (20 G)	Fresh root ginger
1	Garlic clove
3	Scallions
3½ OZ (100 G)	Button mushrooms
3½ OZ (100 G)	Extra-firm tofu
3½ TSP	Light soy sauce
½ TBSP	Sesame oil
½ TSP	Soft light brown sugar
8	Slices of bread
⅓ CUP (50 G)	Sesame seeds (I used black and white)
—	Salt, freshly ground black pepper and vegetable oil

TO SERVE

—	Thai basil, mint and cilantro leaves (optional)
—	Sweet chile sauce (check the label if it needs to be nut-free)

TIP

TO AIR-FRY, SPRAY EACH TOAST WITH VEGETABLE OIL SPRAY AND COOK AT 350°F (180°C) FOR 10 MINUTES, THEN FLIP, SPRAY AGAIN AND COOK FOR ANOTHER 5 MINUTES ON THE OTHER SIDE.

1. Process the nori sheet into very small pieces or tear it with your hands—you want the pieces to be as small as you can get them. Peel the ginger and roughly chop. Roughly chop the garlic, scallions and mushrooms.

2. Wrap the tofu in a clean tea towel and squeeze as much water out of it as you can.

3. Tip the squeezed tofu into a blender or small food processor with the nori, ginger, garlic, scallions and mushrooms. Add the soy sauce, sesame oil and sugar, and blend into a thick paste, scraping down the sides as needed. Add a splash of water if it's too thick. Season with salt and pepper.

4. Using a cookie cutter or glass, cut out a circle from each piece of bread (save the edges of the bread and turn into breadcrumbs for another use). Tip the sesame seeds into a small bowl.

5. Flatten each bread circle slightly. Hold one of the bread circles in your palm to make a taco shape, then carefully fill it with some of the mushroom and tofu mixture.

6. To shallow-fry, pour vegetable oil into a small frying pan to a depth of 1–1½ in (3–4 cm) and place over medium-high heat. To check if the oil is hot enough for frying, drop a small piece of bread into it; if it sizzles immediately, the oil is ready.

7. Carefully lower one of the sesame toasts into the oil and fry for about 2 minutes on each side until golden brown. It will continue to cook after you remove it from the oil, so don't let it get too dark. Dip and roll the open edge (with the exposed filling) of each toast into the sesame seeds, so they stick to it. Set aside on a plate lined with paper towels while you repeat with each toast.

8. Serve the toasts, scattered with the fresh leaves (if using), with sweet chile sauce for dipping.

Musabaha with Zhoug

Musabaha, or warm hummus, is a Middle Eastern dish that is popular in Lebanon, Palestine, Syria and more. It's typically made with whole chickpeas instead of blended, giving it a chunkier texture and richer flavor. It's great at any time of the day, but especially for breakfast.

SERVES 2-4
45 minutes

INGREDIENTS

28 OZ (800 G)	Jar of chickpeas (or 2 × 14 oz/ 400 g cans)
1	Garlic clove
¼ TSP	Ground cumin
1¾ TBSP	Tahini, plus extra to serve
—	Juice of ½ lemon
1 TBSP	Olive oil
1 TBSP	Sumac (optional)
1 TBSP	Sesame seeds
—	Salt and freshly ground black pepper

FOR THE ZHOUG

1½ CUPS (25 G)	Cilantro
¼–½	Red chile (optional)
½	Garlic clove
—	Juice of ½ lemon
⅛ TSP	Ground cumin
2½ TBSP	Olive oil

TIPS

I REALLY RECOMMEND TRYING JARRED CHICKPEAS FOR THIS RECIPE IF YOU CAN FIND THEM. THEY ARE ALWAYS MUCH TASTIER THAN CANNED.

THE ZHOUG WILL KEEP IN AN AIRTIGHT CONTAINER IN THE FRIDGE FOR 4-5 DAYS.

1. Scoop out 1 heaped tablespoon of the chickpeas and set aside for garnish. Empty the remaining chickpeas into a small pot, along with their liquid (aquafaba).

2. Grate the garlic and add to the pot, along with the cumin. Taste before adding salt (some chickpea brands already contain salt).

3. Cook over medium heat for 20-30 minutes, stirring occasionally. Do not let the mixture boil; a very gentle simmer is perfect. The length of time will depend on how hard your chickpeas are (canned ones will need more cooking). You want the chickpeas to be very soft so they melt in your mouth. If the pot looks like it's drying out, add a splash of water.

4. Once the chickpeas are very soft, drain them over a bowl, reserving the cooking water. Pour the chickpeas into a large bowl and stir in the tahini, lemon juice and olive oil, along with a scant ½–⅔ cup (100–150 ml) of the reserved cooking liquid. Stir gently until a creamy tahini sauce forms around the chickpeas. The tahini will seize up when it first comes into contact with the lemon juice, but it will soon begin to loosen. Add more cooking liquid as needed until you have a loose, creamy consistency. Remember that it will become thicker as it cools, as some of the liquid will evaporate, so looser is better. Taste and adjust the seasonings.

5. To make the zhoug, roughly chop the cilantro (removing only the very tough stems) and place in a small food processor. Chop the chile (if using) and the garlic and add these to the food processor too, along with the lemon juice and cumin. Process until you have a chunky mixture. Add a splash of olive oil to help it blend if needed. Stir in the 2½ tablespoons of olive oil and season well with salt and pepper.

6. To serve, pour the warm musabaha into a bowl and top with a drizzle of tahini and a few tablespoons of zhoug. Finish with a sprinkling of sumac, if using, and a scattering of sesame seeds.

● GLUTEN-FREE ● NUT-FREE

Herby Marinated Olives

These olives, inspired by the Persian dish zeytoon parvardeh, showcase the culinary heritage of Iran, where pomegranate with herbs and olives is a distinct combination. It's a perfect balance of sweet, tangy and herby.

SERVES 4
5 minutes

INGREDIENTS

10½ OZ (300 G)	Whole green olives, preferably Greek Halkidiki olives with pits
1 TBSP (5 G)	Mint leaves
5 SPRIGS	Flat-leaf parsley
¼ CUP (5 G)	Cilantro
3 TBSP	Walnuts
1–2	Garlic cloves
1½ TSP	Pomegranate molasses
1 TBSP	Olive oil
—	Salt

1. Drain the olives. Finely chop the herbs and walnuts, and mince the garlic.

2. Combine the olives, herbs, nuts, pomegranate molasses and olive oil in a bowl. Season with salt and mix well, then serve.

Smashed Peas on Toast

These zingy, speedy, crunchy, creamy, protein-packed, gingery peas are everything you want from a toast topping. It's the cheaper, more sustainable, upgraded avocado toast.

SERVES 2
10 minutes

INGREDIENTS

2¼ CUPS (300 G)	Frozen peas
1 TBSP (15 G)	Fresh root ginger
1	Scallion
2 TBSP	Roasted peanuts
3 TBSP	Tahini, plus extra to serve
4	Limes
2	Pieces of wholewheat or sourdough bread
2 TSP	Chile oil or chile flakes
2 TSP	Sesame seeds (optional)
—	Salt and freshly ground black pepper

1. Tip the peas into a heatproof bowl and pour over enough boiling water to cover. Set aside for 5 minutes to defrost.

2. Meanwhile, peel the ginger with the back of a spoon (this removes just the skin) and grate it. Finely slice the green part of the scallion, keeping the white part for another use. Roughly chop the peanuts.

3. Drain the peas and tip into a small food processor, along with the tahini and minced ginger. Squeeze in the juice of 3 of the limes and season with salt and pepper. Process until you get a nice creamy, chunky texture. (If you prefer, you can just do this in a bowl, using a fork to crush the peas and mix everything together.) Taste for seasoning, adding more lime juice if you prefer it more citrusy or more ginger if you like a little heat.

4. Toast your bread, then top each slice with a generous dollop of the pea mixture. Drizzle over some tahini, followed by the chile oil or flakes, then scatter over the peanuts, scallion and sesame seeds, if using. Finish with a final squeeze of lime juice and enjoy.

Smoky Zucchini Dip

Slow-cooking zucchinis like this concentrates the flavor and makes the smokiest, creamiest dip, similar to the eggplant-based baba ganoush. I recommend making extra to stir through pasta the next day with a little pasta water or vegan cream cheese to loosen.

SERVES 2–4
1 hour 40 minutes

INGREDIENTS

6	Zucchinis
2½ TBSP	Tahini, plus extra to serve
—	Juice of 1½ lemons
3 TBSP	Olive oil, plus extra to serve
5 SPRIGS	Flat-leaf parsley
1 TBSP (5 G)	Mint leaves
—	Seeds of 1 pomegranate
—	Pinch of sumac (optional)
—	Sesame seeds (optional)
—	Salt and freshly ground black pepper

1. Preheat the oven to 400°F (200°C).

2. Pierce the zucchinis all over with a fork, then arrange on a roasting pan. Roast for about 1½ hours, or until completely blackened, turning once or twice. The zucchinis should be very soft and should have released most of their water.

3. Remove from the oven and allow to cool. Once cool, carefully slice the zucchinis lengthways and use a spoon to scoop out the flesh into a large bowl. Use a fork to mash the flesh into a chunky purée.

4. Add the tahini, lemon juice and olive oil to the bowl. Season with salt and pepper and stir through. If it's too watery, add a little more tahini, which will thicken it up.

5. Roughly chop the parsley and mint and stir into the dip, saving a little for garnish.

6. Serve the dip in a shallow bowl, topped with a good drizzle of olive oil and a little more tahini. Scatter over the pomegranate seeds and reserved herbs, along with the sumac and sesame seeds, if using.

● GLUTEN-FREE   ● NUT-FREE   ● ALLIUM-FREE

Zesty Chickpea Nori Wrap

I have been making variants of this zingy chickpea filling since I turned vegan 13 years ago and I still crave it all the time. Wrapping it in nori is my favorite way to eat it, but the filling itself is great in a sandwich or a wrap, or piled on top of toast.

SERVES 2
15 minutes

INGREDIENTS

2 × 14 OZ (400 G)	Cans of chickpeas
3	Large nori sheets
½–1 TBSP	Capers
2	Scallions
—	Juice of 2 lemons, (or 1–2 tbsp apple cider vinegar)
2–3 TSP	Dijon mustard
3–4 TBSP	Vegan mayonnaise
—	Pinch of chile flakes, togarashi or chile powder (optional)
1	Head of baby gem or romaine lettuce
—	Salt and freshly ground black pepper

TIPS

SOME BRANDS OF CHICKPEAS ARE SOFTER THAN OTHERS, AND THE HARDER ONES MAY NEED A LITTLE MORE SEASONING, SO START WITH THE SMALLER AMOUNTS OF THE INGREDIENTS AND THEN TASTE AND ADD MORE TO YOUR LIKING.

THESE ARE BEST SERVED IMMEDIATELY ONCE WRAPPED IN THE NORI, BUT THE FILLING WILL KEEP FOR UP TO 3 DAYS IN AN AIRTIGHT CONTAINER IN THE FRIDGE.

1. Drain and rinse the chickpeas and add them to a large bowl.

2. Take one of the nori sheets and shred it into very small pieces (you can either use scissors or just tear it up with your hands; it can be tricky to cut with a knife). Add these pieces to the bowl.

3. Finely chop the capers and scallions and add these to the bowl too. Add the lemon juice (or apple cider vinegar), mustard and mayonnaise, and stir.

4. Use a fork or potato masher to mash the chickpeas into the rest of the ingredients so that about half of the chickpeas are mashed and half are whole. Taste and season well with salt and pepper. Add more lemon juice for acidity, more capers and Dijon for brightness, or more mayo for more creaminess. Add some chile flakes too, if using.

5. To assemble, lay one nori sheet on a chopping board, with the rough side facing up and the faint lines horizontal to you. Take two or three lettuce leaves and press down on the hard stem, cracking it to make it more supple. Lay the lettuce leaves over the nori sheet horizontally (this will stop the nori from getting soggy immediately). Make sure the leaves are close to the edge of the nori that's closest to you.

6. Spoon half of the chickpea mixture over the lettuce and carefully wrap the nori into a roll, like a burrito. Make it as tight as you can without breaking the nori. Wet the far edge of the nori slightly with your fingers to help it stick closed. Repeat with the second wrap.

7. To serve, slice in half with a serrated knife and enjoy.

GLUTEN-FREE

As you might expect from the title, this chapter is packed full of big, nourishing, balanced plates of food. These platters would be great for a dinner party, but are also perfect for meal prep. Some are wonderful sharing side dishes, waiting to be served with one or two others in the chapter, or paired with some of the small plates in Chapter 1. Get creative—and if your eyes are bigger than your stomach, there's always tomorrow.

Szechuan & Peanut Butter Saucy Celeriac Ribbons

I'm always coming up with creative ways to use celeriac, but this is my favorite recipe for the hearty, nutty root veg. The slices emulate noodles, and are served in a biang biang-style sauce—a classic Chinese hand-pulled noodle dish.

SERVES 2–4
1–2 hours

INGREDIENTS

1 LB 12 OZ (800 G)	Celeriac (celery root)
2	Scallions
—	Salt, freshly ground black pepper and olive oil
—	Sesame oil, to serve (optional)

FOR THE SAUCE

1	Shallot
1 TSP	Szechuan peppercorns (see Tip)
2 TSP (10 G)	Fresh root ginger
2	Garlic cloves
3 TBSP	Sunflower oil
1 TSP	Chile flakes
1 TBSP	Tomato paste
2 TBSP	Sesame seeds (use a mix of black and white if you can), plus extra to serve
2 TBSP	Smooth peanut butter

TIPS

IF YOU CAN'T FIND OR DON'T LIKE SZECHUAN PEPPERCORNS, SWAP THEM FOR MORE CHILE FLAKES OR LEAVE THEM OUT; THE SAUCE WILL STILL BE DELICIOUS.

YOU CAN COOK THE CELERIAC UP TO 2 DAYS IN ADVANCE AND KEEP IT REFRIGERATED WHOLE. WHEN YOU'RE READY TO SERVE, SLICE THE CELERIAC AND LAY THE SLICES ON A BAKING SHEET TO GENTLY WARM THROUGH IN THE OVEN.

1. Preheat the oven to 410°F (210°C).

2. Wash the celeriac(s) well and cut off any knobbly bits with dirt that you can't get to. If you're using one large celeriac, cut it in half to reduce the cooking time. Drizzle with olive oil and season with plenty of salt and pepper, rubbing it all over the surface. Wrap tightly in foil and place on a baking sheet.

3. Roast the celeriac in the oven for 1–1½ hours until cooked through. Poke a skewer into the center to test—there should be no resistance. If in doubt, cook for longer, as it's much better to overcook than undercook them. Leave to cool completely.

4. Once cooled, thinly slice the celeriac with a knife or mandolin. Don't worry if some breaks; the texture will add to the dish.

5. Now make the sauce. Thinly slice the shallot. Grind or crush the Szechuan peppercorns. Peel and finely grate the ginger, and finely chop the garlic.

6. Heat the sunflower oil in a small saucepan over low-medium heat. Add the shallot, along with the Szechuan peppercorns, ginger, garlic and chile flakes. Season with a good pinch of salt and fry for 10–12 minutes, until the shallot has softened but not browned and the mixture is smelling very aromatic. Stir frequently and reduce the heat if the shallot starts to crisp, then stir in the tomato paste and sesame seeds and cook for 3–5 minutes, then take off the heat.

7. Add the peanut butter to the pan, along with a scant 1 cup (200 ml) of boiling water, and stir to combine. Season to taste.

8. Chop the scallions into three equal pieces, then thinly slice each one lengthways so you are left with very thin batons. To serve, spoon three-quarters of the sauce on a large platter or in a wide bowl. Layer the celeriac on top and drizzle the remaining sauce over. Top with a drizzle of sesame oil, if using, along with more sesame seeds and the scallion batons.

● GLUTEN-FREE

Black Rice with Sticky Carrots & Citrus

Black rice has a distinct nutty flavor and chewy texture that's so worth hunting down if you've never tried it. It has higher levels of fiber, minerals and vitamins compared to white rice, and the deep purple hue is attributed to the high level of antioxidants. If you can't find it, though, brown rice or any other whole grain will make a great base for these sticky, citrusy veggies.

SERVES 3–4 AS A MAIN OR 4–6 AS A SIDE
45 minutes

INGREDIENTS

2¼ CUPS (400 G)	Black rice
1 LB (500 G)	Carrots
1	Small red onion
2	Mandarins (or clementines or tangerines)
1	Lemon, plus wedges
1 CUP (200 G)	Canned chickpeas
3 TBSP	Maple syrup
5 TBSP	Olive oil, plus extra to serve
4 TBSP	Tahini
—	Handful of pistachios
—	Salt and freshly ground black pepper

FOR THE VINAIGRETTE

—	Zest of 2 mandarins (or clementines or tangerines)
3½ TBSP	Mandarin juice (or clementines or tangerines)
5 TBSP	Apple cider vinegar
½ TBSP	Maple syrup
1½ TBSP	Olive oil

1. Preheat the oven to 425°F (220°C).

2. Rinse the rice and tip it into a saucepan with plenty of water. Bring to a boil, then reduce the heat to low and simmer for 20 minutes until tender. Drain, then tip it back into the pan and cover with a tea towel.

3. Scrub the carrots and quarter them lengthways. Slice the onion into eighths, keeping the stem intact. Slice the mandarins and lemon into thin rounds (remove any seeds). Drain the chickpeas.

4. Combine the onion, carrots, chickpeas, and mandarin and lemon slices on a large baking sheet. Pour over the maple syrup and olive oil, then season with salt and pepper and toss to coat.

5. Roast for 25–30 minutes, tossing once or twice, until the carrots are tender and starting to char and the citrus is soft and caramelized.

6. Meanwhile, make the rice vinaigrette. Add all the ingredients to a jug and season to taste with salt and pepper. Whisk to combine and pour over the warm rice, then stir well. Taste and adjust, adding more citrus, vinegar or salt to your liking.

7. In a small bowl, whisk the tahini with a scant ½ cup (100 ml) of cold water until smooth, and season with a sprinkle of salt and pepper.

8. To plate, pour three-quarters of the tahini sauce onto a large platter (or two). Ladle over the rice and top with the roasted veg. Finish with a squeeze of citrus, a drizzle of olive oil and the rest of the tahini.

9. Sprinkle over the pistachios, then serve.

Cauliflower with Harissa Tahini & Lentils

Cauliflower, lentils, tahini and harissa are among my favorite combinations. This is also one of my favorite ways to cook lentils, with flavor and texture from the spices, garlic and onions. Altogether, it's a delicious dish, and you can serve it with rice to make it a complete meal.

SERVES 2-4
45 minutes

INGREDIENTS

1¼ CUPS (250 G)	Puy lentils (or any other small green or black lentils)
2	Onions
3 TBSP	Olive oil, plus extra for drizzling
1 TSP	Coriander seeds (or ¾ tsp ground coriander)
1 TSP	Cumin seeds (or ¾ tsp ground cumin)
3-4	Garlic cloves
1-2 TBSP	Sherry vinegar
2	Small cauliflowers
2 TBSP	Za'atar (optional)
½ CUP (50 G)	Pistachios (optional)
–	Salt and ground black pepper

FOR THE TAHINI SAUCE

¼ CUP (65 G)	Tahini
2 TBSP	Harissa paste
–	Splash of sherry vinegar

TIPS

TO MAKE THE CAULIFLOWER IN AN AIR FRYER, DRIZZLE WITH OIL AND AIR-FRY THE FLORETS AT 375°F (190°C) FOR 10 MINUTES, AND THE LEAVES AT 350°F (180°C) FOR 3 MINUTES.

IF YOU'RE PREPPING THIS IN ADVANCE, KEEP THE TAHINI SAUCE SEPARATE UNTIL YOU'RE READY TO SERVE.

1. Preheat the oven to 400°F (200°C).

2. Rinse the lentils well and add to a saucepan. Cover with plenty of water and bring to a boil. Cook until al dente (3 minutes less than package instructions) and drain.

3. Meanwhile, finely slice the onions. Heat a drizzle of olive oil in a large pan over medium heat. Add the onions and some salt, and sauté for 15–20 minutes until soft and jammy. Take the time to really soften the onions here to get the most flavor.

4. If using coriander and cumin seeds, lightly crush them in a mortar and pestle. Mince the garlic. Add the coriander and cumin to the onions, along with the garlic, and cook for 2–3 minutes, until fragrant. Add the cooked lentils and 2–3 tablespoons of water, and cook for 5–8 minutes until the lentils are cooked but still firm. Deglaze the pan with the sherry vinegar, stir well and season with plenty of salt and pepper.

5. Remove the leaves from the cauliflowers and set aside. Chop them into small pieces, including the stem. Put on a baking sheet and drizzle with the olive oil. Season with salt and pepper and sprinkle with za'atar, if using, then toss to coat. Roast for 25 minutes until golden and crisp. Remove tough, large stems from the cauliflower leaves, then toss in a little oil and season. Add to the pan for the final 8–10 minutes and roast until crispy.

6. To make the tahini sauce, whisk together the tahini and ½–⅔ cup (120–150 ml) cold water. It will be thick, but don't worry—keep whisking and adding water until it has a creamy consistency. Add the harissa and sherry vinegar, then season with salt and pepper, taste and adjust if necessary. Some brands of tahini are quite bitter; if that's the case, add more acidity (vinegar or lemon) and/or sweetness (agave or maple syrup). Serve the lentils on a plate with the cauliflower on top, and a good drizzle of tahini sauce. Finish with the pistachios, if using.

• GLUTEN-FREE

Crispy Kale & Brussels Sprouts Salad

This salad is full of textures and flavors—crispy kale and shredded sprouts, nutty pecans and a pop of pomegranate seeds, all tied together with a punchy, creamy dressing. If Brussels sprouts are not in season, swap them out for more kale.

SERVES 2
30 minutes

INGREDIENTS

12 OZ (350 G)	Brussels sprouts
7 OZ (200 G)	Kale
⅔ CUP (75 G)	Pecans
—	Seeds of 1 pomegranate
—	Salt, freshly ground black pepper and olive oil

FOR THE DRESSING

3 TBSP	Vegan mayonnaise
½ TBSP	White miso paste
½ TBSP	Wholegrain mustard
—	Juice of ½ lemon
½ TSP	Maple syrup

1. Preheat the oven to 410°F (210°C).

2. Wash the sprouts and remove any black outer leaves, then wash the kale and remove the very tough stems.

3. Finely slice the sprouts and place on a baking sheet. Drizzle with olive oil and season well with salt and pepper. Bake for 20–25 minutes until crispy, tossing once or twice to ensure they bake evenly.

4. Tear the kale into bite-sized pieces and spread out on another baking sheet. Drizzle with olive oil and season well with salt and pepper. Bake for 15 minutes on the lower rack until crispy, tossing once or twice to ensure the leaves bake evenly.

5. Spread the pecans on a small baking sheet and bake for 7–10 minutes, until toasted and fragrant. Roughly chop and set aside.

6. Meanwhile, in a small bowl or jug, whisk the dressing ingredients until well combined. Season with salt and pepper, taste and adjust as you like.

7. To assemble the salad, combine the kale, sprouts and half of the pecans and pomegranate seeds with the dressing. Toss to coat, then finish by sprinkling over the rest of the pomegranate seeds and pecans. Best served fresh while it's crispy.

● GLUTEN-FREE   ● ALLIUM-FREE

Crushed Spiced Squash with Hazelnut Gremolata

Gently crushing roasted veggies, like this squash, is a great way to create a new texture; think of it like a chunky mash. It's a perfect way to use up leftover roasted root veg. The hazelnut gremolata adds a little flavor boost, while the giant couscous and a few spoons of yogurt complete the meal. This dish is lovely hot or cold and makes a great packed lunch.

SERVES 2 AS A MAIN, 4 AS A SIDE
45 minutes

INGREDIENTS

1	Small butternut squash (1 lb 10 oz/750 g)
1 TSP	Fennel seeds
1 TSP	Coriander seeds
1 TSP	Cumin seeds
½ TSP	Ground ginger
½ TSP	Smoked paprika
3 TBSP	Olive oil, plus extra to serve
14 OZ (400 G)	Can of chickpeas
1⅓ CUPS (200 G)	Giant couscous (or use brown rice or another whole grain)
½ CUP (100 G)	Plain vegan yogurt (or soy or oat)
¼ TBSP	Chile flakes (optional)
—	Salt and freshly ground black pepper

FOR THE HAZELNUT GREMOLATA

3 TBSP	Hazelnuts
1	Big garlic clove
⅔ CUP (40 G)	Flat-leaf parsley
1	Lemon
5 TBSP	Olive oil

TIPS

YOU CAN ROAST THE SQUASH SKIN AND SEEDS AND USE THEM TO ADD EXTRA TEXTURE TO THIS DISH, OR JUST ENJOY THEM AS A SNACK (SEE PAGE 142).

1. Preheat the oven to 425°F (220°C).

2. Peel and halve the squash and remove the seeds (see Tip). Cut it into ¾ in (2 cm) cubes and spread on a large roasting pan.

3. Combine the fennel, coriander and cumin seeds in a mortar with the ginger and paprika, and grind into rough crumbs. Sprinkle this over the squash, then add 2 tablespoons of the olive oil. Season well with salt and pepper and toss to combine.

4. Roast the squash for 15 minutes, then drain the chickpeas and add them to the roasting pan, along with the remaining tablespoon of olive oil. Mix well and roast for another 15 minutes until the squash is soft and starting to char in places.

5. Meanwhile, cook your couscous in a saucepan of boiling water for 8 minutes. Drain and rinse quickly to prevent it sticking.

6. To make the gremolata, lightly toast the hazelnuts in a dry frying pan. Mince the garlic and roughly chop the parsley. Zest and juice the lemon, reserving the zest for later. Add the lemon juice, garlic, parsley, hazelnuts and 2 tablespoons of the olive oil to a small food processor and pulse until you have chunky paste. Pour this into a bowl and add the remaining 3 tablespoons of olive oil. Season with salt and pepper to taste. The mixture should be bright, zesty and crunchy.

7. Once the squash is cooked, use a fork or a potato masher to mash about half to three-quarters of the squash and chickpeas in the pan you cooked them in.

8. Pour the couscous into a large bowl or platter and mix in the crushed squash mixture. Add the gremolata and a the yogurt. Finish with the reserved lemon zest, a sprinkle of chile flakes, and a final drizzle of olive oil, if you like.

Masala-Spiced Chickpeas & Couscous

There are a few elements in this dish, but it comes together surprisingly easily to make a hearty, healthy weeknight meal. This one is a delicious dinner or lunch and perfect to double up quantities for meal prep.

SERVES 2
35 minutes

INGREDIENTS

½ CUP (100 G)	Couscous
1 CUP (15 G)	Cilantro
—	Salt, freshly ground black pepper and olive oil

FOR THE MAPLE PISTACHIOS (OPTIONAL)

¼ CUP (30 G)	Pistachios
1 TSP	Vegan butter
1 TSP	Maple syrup

FOR THE GARLIC MUSHROOMS

1	Small onion
3	Garlic cloves
3½ OZ (100 G)	Kale
10½ OZ (300 G)	Crimini mushrooms

FOR THE CUMIN YOGURT

½ CUP (100 G)	Plain vegan yogurt
—	Pinch of ground cumin
½ TBSP	Tahini (optional)
—	Juice of 1 lemon, plus extra to serve

FOR THE MASALA-SPICED CHICKPEAS

1	Small onion
4	Garlic cloves
2 TSP (8 G)	Fresh root ginger (optional)
28 OZ (800 G)	Can of chickpeas
2 TSP	Garam masala
½ TSP	Ground cumin

1. Tip the couscous into a heatproof bowl. Pour over ⅔ cup (150 ml) of boiling water, along with ½ teaspoon of olive oil, and mix well with a fork. Cover the bowl with a plate and set aside to steam.

2. If you are making the maple pistachios, heat a small frying pan over medium heat. Add the pistachios and butter to the pan and swirl around for 4–5 minutes until the butter has melted and the pistachios have browned. Finally, add the maple syrup and a sprinkle of salt, and stir with a wooden spoon to combine. Remove from the heat and let them cool. They will harden as they cool.

3. To make the garlic mushrooms, finely slice the onion and mince the garlic. Remove any tough stems from the kale. Slice the mushrooms into thick slices.

4. Heat a good drizzle of olive oil in a large frying pan over medium heat. Add the onion and a little salt and cook, stirring occasionally, for 5–6 minutes until translucent. Add the mushrooms and garlic. Fry for 5 minutes, then add the kale. Season well with salt and pepper and add a little more oil if needed. Cook for another few minutes until the mushrooms are cooked and caramelized in places and the kale is cooked through.

5. While the mushrooms are cooking, make the cumin yogurt. In a bowl, combine the yogurt with the cumin and a pinch of salt in a bowl. Add the tahini, if using, and a squeeze of lemon juice. Taste and adjust to your liking, adding more lemon juice, cumin, or salt as needed.

6. Remove the mushrooms from the frying pan and set aside in a bowl. Wipe the pan clean.

7. The couscous should be cooked by now—check on it and fluff it up with a fork.

CONTINUED OVERLEAF

RECIPE CONTINUED

8. For the masala-spiced chickpeas, dice the onion, mince the garlic and grate the ginger, if using. Heat a drizzle of olive oil in the now-empty frying pan over medium-high heat. Add the diced onion and fry for 4–5 minutes, then add the ginger and garlic and stir-fry for another minute or so. Drain the chickpeas and add them to the pan, along with 1 tablespoon of olive oil and the garam masala and cumin. Now stir in the couscous. Season generously with salt and pepper and cook for about 5 minutes until starting to brown in places, stirring occasionally. Take off the heat.

9. Finely chop the cilantro and stir it through the couscous and chickpeas. Roughly chop the maple pistachios, if using.

10. To assemble, heap the spiced chickpeas and couscous onto a plate, then top with the garlic mushrooms and a big spoonful of the cumin yogurt. Sprinkle over the maple pistachios and squeeze over plenty of lemon to serve.

Spicy Mushroom Skewers with Peanut Lime Sauce

This dish is very easy to love: spicy, charred, marinated mushrooms with a creamy, limey peanut sauce, rounded out with fluffy rice and edamame for protein and fiber. This is both a weeknight favorite and one that will impress your guests.

**SERVES 2 AS A MAIN,
4 AS PART OF A SPREAD**

45 minutes

INGREDIENTS

14 OZ (400 G)	Mixed mushrooms (king oyster, oyster, shiitake or portobello work well)
1	Red chile (optional)
3	Scallions
1 TBSP	Olive oil
2½ TBSP	Roasted peanuts (optional)

FOR THE MARINADE

1½ TBSP (20 G)	Fresh root ginger
2	Garlic cloves
1–2	Red chiles
⅓ CUP (85 ML)	Light soy sauce (or tamari if gluten-free)
3½ TBSP	Maple syrup or agave
2 TBSP	Toasted sesame oil

FOR THE PEANUT LIME SAUCE

1	Small garlic clove
1 TBSP	Light soy sauce (or tamari if gluten-free)
3 TBSP	Crunchy peanut butter
1 TBSP	Maple syrup
—	Juice of 1 lime
1 TBSP	Sesame oil
—	Salt and freshly ground black pepper

FOR THE RICE

¾ CUP (170 G)	Jasmine rice
½ CUP (80 G)	Shelled edamame beans, fresh or frozen (defrosted if frozen)

1. Slice the king oyster mushrooms lengthways into ¼ in (5 mm) strips. Pull the oyster mushrooms into large strips and chop any other mushrooms into bite-sized pieces.

2. To make the marinade, grate the ginger and mince the garlic and chiles (discarding the seeds). Mix these with the rest of the marinade ingredients in a mixing bowl. Alternatively, throw all the marinade ingredients into a blender and blend until smooth.

3. Combine the mushrooms with the marinade in a shallow bowl or container. Toss a few times to make sure the mushrooms are evenly coated. Set aside to marinate while you prepare the rest of the dish (if you like, you can do this the day before and leave them to marinate overnight).

4. To make the peanut lime sauce, grate the garlic into a small bowl, then add all the other ingredients, along with ½ tablespoon water. Mix well to combine, adding a little more water if needed. Taste and adjust the seasonings to your liking.

5. Rinse the rice thoroughly under cold running water, then tip into a saucepan. Add a scant 1½ cups (340 ml) of water to the pan, then cover with a lid and bring to a boil over high heat. As soon as it's boiling, reduce the heat to medium and cook for 5 minutes, then reduce the heat to low and gently simmer for another 5 minutes. Remove from the heat and leave to stand, with the lid on, for 5 minutes more. Now remove the lid and fluff up the rice with a fork. It should be perfectly cooked.

6. Add the edamame beans to the rice and stir through.

CONTINUED OVERLEAF

● GLUTEN-FREE

TIP

YOU WILL NEED SKEWERS FOR THIS RECIPE; IF YOU ARE USING WOODEN ONES, SOAK THEM IN WATER FOR AT LEAST 5 MINUTES BEFORE YOU BEGIN. ALTERNATIVELY, YOU CAN STIR-FRY THE MUSHROOMS INSTEAD OF SKEWERING, IF YOU PREFER.

RECIPE CONTINUED

7   Next, prepare the mushrooms for cooking. Divide the mushrooms among four skewers, folding any mushroom strips. Slice the chile, if using. Chop two of the scallions into four pieces each and add a scallion piece to each skewer tip, along with an optional slice of chile.

8   Heat a griddle pan or non-stick frying pan over medium heat. Brush the mushroom skewers with the olive oil, then sear for 2–3 minutes on each side until charred and cooked through.

9   Finely slice the remaining scallion and chop the peanuts, if using.

10 Tip the rice onto a large platter. Top with the mushroom skewers, then scatter over the finely sliced scallions, remaining chile, and peanuts, if using. Serve with the sauce drizzled over or on the side.

Grilled Lettuce with Orange Sauce & Smoky Tofu Crisp

Grilling lettuce unlocks an earthy, smoky, almost nutty sweetness that takes the humble leaf to a new level. All the elements in this recipe are winners in their own right, but combining the lettuce with the salty, crispy tofu crumbs, the bright and zesty sauce and the pop of pickled shallots makes this dish an explosion of flavor and texture.

SERVES 4 AS A SIDE
25 minutes

INGREDIENTS

6	Baby gem lettuces
–	Salt, freshly ground black pepper and olive oil
–	Lemon wedges, to serve

FOR THE PICKLED SHALLOT

1	Shallot
2 TBSP	Lemon juice
½ TSP	Sugar
¼ TSP	Fine salt

FOR THE ORANGE CARROT SAUCE

3½ OZ (100 G)	Carrots
½ TBSP	Miso paste
1 TBSP	Orange juice
2 TSP (10 G)	Fresh root ginger
1 TSP	Sherry vinegar
1 TSP	Maple syrup
2½ TBSP	Vegan mayonnaise

FOR THE TOFU CRISP

5½ OZ (150 G)	Extra-firm tofu
2 TBSP	Olive oil
½ TSP	Smoked paprika
2 TSP	Light soy sauce (or tamari if gluten-free)
2½ TSP	Black sesame seeds

TIP
FOR A VARIATION, TRY THIS WITH BOK CHOI INSTEAD OF LETTUCE.

1. Begin with the pickled shallot. Thinly slice the shallot into rounds and place in a bowl with the rest of the ingredients. Set aside to pickle for at least 15 minutes (up to 1 hour), then drain, squeezing out the liquid.

2. To make the sauce, peel and finely chop the carrots. Add to a high-speed blender with all the other ingredients and 2 tablespoons of water, and blend until smooth.

3. To make the tofu crisp, grate the tofu. Heat the olive oil in a large grill pan or frying pan over medium heat. Add the grated tofu and paprika, and fry for 5–8 minutes until starting to brown. Add the soy sauce and sesame seeds, and fry for another 3–5 minutes until very crispy. Transfer to a plate and set aside.

4. Wipe the pan clean for the lettuce and place over medium-high heat. Slice the lettuces in half and brush the cut sides with a little olive oil, then sprinkle with salt and pepper. Add the lettuce halves to the hot pan, cut-sides down, and cook for 4–5 minutes, pressing them down to get an even char. When finished, slice each piece in half again lengthways.

5. To assemble, pour the sauce onto a large plate or platter. Pile up the lettuce on top, followed by the pickled shallot and crispy tofu. Serve with a good squeeze of lemon.

● GLUTEN-FREE ● NUT-FREE

Pointed Cabbage with Sesame Whipped Butter Beans

Cabbage comes to life when it's roasted, and serving it with creamy whipped butter beans and these crunchy miso cashews really elevates the delicious pointed cabbage. To make this a main, serve with a grain like wild rice, farro or freekeh.

SERVES 2 AS A MAIN, 4 AS A SIDE
30 minutes

INGREDIENTS

2	Pointed cabbages
–	Salt, freshly ground black pepper and olive oil
–	Handful of cilantro (optional), chopped, to serve
1	Scallion (optional), sliced, to serve

FOR THE SESAME WHIPPED BUTTER BEANS

2 × 14 OZ (400 G)	Cans of butter beans
1	Garlic clove
2 TBSP	Sesame oil
⅓ CUP (75 ML)	Lemon juice
2 TBSP	Tahini
½ TSP	Flaky sea salt

FOR THE MISO CASHEW BUTTER

⅔ CUP (70 G)	Cashews
7 TBSP (100 G)	Vegan butter (ideally the type that comes in a block wrapped in paper)
1–2 TBSP	Miso paste

1. Preheat the oven to 425°F (220°C) and line a baking sheet with parchment paper.

2. Cut the cabbages into quarters (or eighths if they are very big) and drizzle with olive oil. Season with salt and pepper and rub it all in, making sure the cabbage wedges are seasoned all over and in between the leaves as much as possible.

3. Arrange the pieces cut-side up on the prepared pan and roast for 15–18 minutes until nicely charred on top. Use a small knife to check if the cabbage is cooked at the thickest part; it should pierce through easily. If not, cover the wedges with foil and pop the pan back into the oven for another 5–8 minutes, then check again.

4. Meanwhile, make the whipped butter beans. Drain the butter beans over a bowl and keep the liquid from the cans (this is aquafaba). Measure out ½ cup (120 ml) of the aquafaba and add it to a blender with the butter beans and the remaining ingredients. Blend until smooth, then taste and adjust the seasoning.

5. To make the miso cashew butter, roughly chop the cashews. Melt the butter in a small saucepan over low heat. Once melted, add the cashews and cook for about 10 minutes, stirring often, until the cashews are golden and the butter starts to brown. The butter will froth up; that's OK, just keep stirring it. Once the cashews are toasted and crunchy, remove from the heat. Stir through 1 tablespoon of the miso, which will melt into the butter from the residual heat. Taste and add more miso if you like. Once it's to your liking, pour the mixture into a bowl to stop it from cooking further.

6. To assemble, spread the whipped butter beans over a large platter. Lay the cabbage wedges over the top and drizzle over the miso cashew butter. Finish with the chopped cilantro and scallion, if using, and serve.

Miso Eggplant on Herby Rice Noodles

Eggplant can be divisive, but when cooked right it has an unctuous, firm, yet creamy texture. Made by salting the eggplants, introducing a temperature change, and using a miso glaze, these are so delicious they will convert any sceptics.

SERVES 2 AS A MAIN, 4 AS A SIDE
40 minutes

INGREDIENTS

2	Large eggplants
—	Salt, black pepper and olive oil

FOR THE GLAZE

2½ TBSP	White miso paste
3 TBSP	Agave (or maple syrup)
4 TSP	Sesame oil
1 TBSP	Japanese rice vinegar
⅓ CUP (50 G)	White sesame seeds

FOR THE SALAD

5½ OZ (150 G)	Vermicelli rice noodles
½	White cabbage or 1 small pointed cabbage (about 1 lb 5 oz/600 g)
1–2	Red chiles
2	Scallions
⅓ CUP (50 G)	Roasted peanuts
2 CUPS (30 G)	Cilantro leaves
¼ CUP (20 G)	Mint leaves
½ CUP (20 G)	Basil leaves

FOR THE SALAD DRESSING

1½ TBSP (20 G)	Fresh root ginger
2	Garlic cloves
2½ TBSP	Light or dark soy sauce
3½ TBSP	Rice vinegar
3½ TBSP	Agave (or maple syrup)
3½ TBSP	Sunflower oil
2 TBSP	Sesame oil
—	Juice of 3 limes
1 TBSP	Miso paste

1. Preheat the oven to 470°F (240°C) and line a baking sheet with parchment paper.

2. Cut each eggplant into eight wedges and place in a large bowl or colander. Sprinkle over ½ tablespoon of salt and leave for at least 10 minutes to remove some of the moisture and bitterness.

3. While you wait, make the miso glaze. In a small bowl, simply whisk together the glaze ingredients until well combined.

4. After 10 minutes, use a paper towel to wipe the salt and moisture off the eggplants, then arrange the wedges on the prepared baking sheet. Drizzle with a little olive oil and season with salt and pepper. Roast for 15 minutes, then remove the eggplants from the oven and generously brush with the miso glaze. Reduce the heat to 410°F (210°C) and roast for another 12–15 minutes until starting to brown and char in spots. Turn off the oven and keep the eggplants in there with the door slightly open to stay warm while you prepare the rest of the dish.

5. To make the salad, cook the rice noodles according to the package instructions. Drain and rinse under cold water to prevent from sticking, then place in a large bowl. Finely slice the cabbage, chile(s) and scallions and add to the bowl. Roughly chop the peanuts and herbs and add them too.

6. To make the dressing, use a small spoon to peel the skin off the ginger. Finely grate the ginger and garlic into a small bowl, then add the rest of the dressing ingredients. Alternatively, you can add everything to a blender and blend until smooth.

7. Pour the dressing over the salad and toss well. Taste and adjust the seasonings if needed.

8. To serve, spread out the salad on a large platter and pile the miso eggplants on top.

Tangy New Potato Salad

I love potato salads and I really love vegan mayonnaise. But I wanted to make a crisp, fresh potato salad that doesn't rely on mayo, so here it is: a healthy iteration with added greens that still packs a tangy punch.

SERVES 4
35 minutes

INGREDIENTS

2 LB 4 OZ (1 KG)	New potatoes
⅓ CUP (50 G)	Walnuts
7 OZ (200 G)	Broccolini
1 TSP	Chile flakes (optional)
—	Salt and freshly ground black pepper

FOR THE DRESSING

2	Small garlic cloves
—	Zest and juice of 1 lemon
5 TBSP	Olive oil
1½ TBSP	Capers
1 TSP	Dried oregano

1. Preheat the oven to 400°F (200°C).

2. Bring a big pot of water to a boil with plenty of salt. Add the potatoes and boil for 15–18 minutes until just fork tender. Keep checking them frequently after 14 minutes. Drain and leave them in a colander to steam dry.

3. Spread out the walnuts on a baking sheet and toast in the oven for 5–8 minutes until golden. Once cool enough to handle, roughly chop them and set aside.

4. Remove any tough ends from the broccoli. Bring another pot of salted water to a boil, then add the broccoli and cook for 2 minutes. Drain and immediately run the broccoli under very cold water or dunk it into an ice bath to stop it cooking further.

5. To make the dressing, grate the garlic into a large salad bowl, then add the remaining dressing ingredients. Whisk to combine and season with plenty of salt and pepper.

6. Chop the broccoli into ½–¾ in (1–2 cm) pieces and the potatoes into quarters. Add to the bowl and toss to coat in the dressing. Taste and add more lemon, salt or pepper to your liking.

7. Top the warm salad with the chopped walnuts and a sprinkle of chile flakes, if using.

● GLUTEN-FREE

Roasted Zucchinis with Lemony Whipped Tofu

In this book, there are lots of recipes with simple elements that come together to make a dish pop. I also want you to see how versatile each individual element is, so you can use them creatively on your own. This whipped tofu is the perfect example, as it comes together in no time and you can use it anywhere you'd like a tangy, creamy addition and to level up your protein.

SERVES 2
25 minutes

INGREDIENTS

2	Zucchinis
4 TBSP	Olive oil
1 TBSP (5 G)	Mint leaves, plus extra to serve
¼ CUP (10 G)	Basil leaves, plus extra to serve
2 TSP	Capers, plus extra to serve
—	Salt and freshly ground black pepper

FOR THE WHIPPED TOFU

10½ OZ (300 G)	Medium-firm tofu
—	Juice of 2 lemons, plus extra to serve
1 TBSP	Olive oil
2 TSP	White miso paste (optional)
3 TBSP	Nutritional yeast
¼ TSP	Garlic powder

TO SERVE

—	Your choice of cooked grain (white or brown rice, quinoa, spelt or farro would all be great)
—	Pomegranate molasses (or date syrup)
3 TBSP	Toasted pine nuts or sunflower seeds

1. For the whipped tofu, add all the ingredients to a high-speed blender and blend until smooth. Season to taste.

2. Preheat the broiler to high and line a baking sheet with parchment paper.

3. Cut the zucchinis into ½ in (1.5 cm) rounds. Place them in a large bowl and drizzle over 2 tablespoons of the olive oil. Season well with salt and pepper, then toss to coat. Arrange the zucchini slices on the prepared pan and place under the broiler for 6–8 minutes, then flip and cook for another 4–5 minutes on the other side until golden and crispy in patches.

4. Meanwhile, roughly chop the herbs. Add the capers to the chopping board, and a pinch of salt, and keep chopping the herbs and capers together until you have a rough paste. Scrape into a large bowl with the remaining 2 tablespoons of olive oil and season with a few twists of pepper.

5. While the zucchinis are still warm, tip them into the bowl with the herby mix and toss to coat. Season to taste.

6. To serve, spread the whipped tofu across a plate and layer over your cooked grains and the herby zucchinis. Finish with a drizzle of pomegranate molasses, a squeeze of lemon juice and some pine nuts or sunflower seeds, along with a few extra capers and herbs.

● NUT-FREE

Herby Smacked Cucumber Salad with Tahini & Chile Oil

The word "salad" might make you think of bland bowls of limp leaves, but it shouldn't. This is my idea of a salad: layers of texture, fresh flavors, a punchy, balanced dressing and always a crunchy sprinkle to finish.

SERVES 2-4
25 minutes

INGREDIENTS

2	Large cucumbers
1	Baby gem lettuce
¼ CUP (40 G)	Roasted peanuts
1¾ OZ (50 G)	Radishes (optional)
1 CUP (15 G)	Cilantro leaves
¼ CUP (10 G)	Basil leaves
2 TBSP (10 G)	Mint leaves
2 TBSP	Crispy chile oil
2 TBSP	Sesame seeds (optional)
–	Salt and freshly ground black pepper

FOR THE DRESSING

1-3	Bird's eye chiles (or a less spicy red chile, if you prefer)
2	Large garlic cloves
2 TBSP	Light soy sauce
2 TBSP	Sesame oil
4 TSP	Rice vinegar

FOR THE TAHINI SAUCE

½ CUP (100 ML)	Tahini
–	Juice of 1 lemon
1 TBSP	Sesame oil
1 TBSP	Light soy sauce

1. Trim the tips of the cucumbers then, using a rolling pin, smash them individually until they are partly flattened. Slice each one lengthways into thick strips and scoop out the soft seeds.

2. Place the cucumber strips in a colander set over a bowl and season with salt and pepper. Toss well, then set aside to drain for at least 15 minutes. This will help remove some of the water content, which will later allow the cucumbers to absorb more of the dressing.

3. To make the dressing, slice the chile(s), keeping some aside for garnish, and mince the garlic. Combine these in a bowl with the soy sauce, sesame oil and rice vinegar. Whisk well and set aside.

4. Next, make the tahini sauce. Combine all the ingredients in a small bowl with 6 tablespoons of water and whisk to combine.

5. Roughly chop the baby gem lettuce and the peanuts, and finely slice the radishes, if using.

6. Once the cucumbers have been draining for 15 minutes, give them a good toss, then slice into ¾ in (2 cm) slices on the diagonal. Tip them into a large bowl, along with the dressing, lettuce, radishes and most of the herbs (keep some for garnish), then toss well.

7. Pour the tahini sauce onto a large platter. Use your hands or a slotted spoon to arrange the salad on top of the tahini sauce. Finish with a drizzle of chile oil, then the rest of the herbs and reserved chile, and finally the peanuts and sesame seeds, if using. Best enjoyed immediately.

Smashed Potatoes with Spicy Tomato Sauce

Crispy, seasoned smashed potatoes are the perfect vessel to dip into this slightly spicy red sauce.

SERVES 4–6 AS A SIDE
1 hour

INGREDIENTS

2 LB 4 OZ (1 KG)	New potatoes
5 TBSP	Za'atar (or a mix of dried herbs, such as an Italian blend)
5–7 TBSP	Olive oil
—	Salt and freshly ground black pepper

FOR THE SAUCE

1 LB (460 G)	Jar of roasted red peppers
6	Large garlic cloves
2 TBSP	Olive oil
1 TBSP	Smoked paprika
½ TSP	Chile flakes
½–1 TSP	Cayenne pepper
1 TBSP	Tomato paste
1 TBSP	Balsamic vinegar
28 OZ (800 G)	Can of chopped tomatoes

1. Preheat the oven to 425°F (220°C).

2. Bring a big pot of water to a boil with plenty of salt. Add the potatoes and boil for 20–25 minutes until just soft enough to pierce with a fork.

3. Drain the potatoes and spread them out on a large baking sheet. Use a glass to gently smash the potatoes. Don't press too hard; they should be partly crushed, but still intact.

4. In a small bowl, mix the za'atar and the olive oil with a little salt and pepper. Brush some of the oil generously over the potatoes and roast for 15 minutes, then flip them over and brush with the rest of the oil. Roast for another 15–20 minutes until perfectly crispy.

5. Meanwhile, make the sauce. Drain the peppers, then chop them into small pieces. Mince the garlic.

6. Heat the olive oil in a medium-sized frying pan over medium heat. Add the garlic and peppers and fry for 3–4 minutes, then stir in all the spices and the tomato paste. Fry for 2 minutes, stirring often, then add the balsamic vinegar and canned tomatoes. Reduce the heat to low and cover, with the lid slightly ajar. Cook for 45 minutes, stirring often to make sure it doesn't catch at the bottom of the pan, until the sauce is thick and reduced. Taste and season well.

7. Spread the sauce onto a large dish or plate and pile the crispy potatoes on top to serve.

● GLUTEN-FREE   ● NUT-FREE

Farinata with Romesco, Broccolini & Edamame

Farinata is a simple savory pancake made with chickpea flour, water, olive oil, salt and sometimes herbs. You can whip one up in minutes to add protein and fiber to any leftover sauces or veggies—I've topped this one with a creamy romesco sauce and roasted broccolini. This is a versatile recipe to have on rotation, and I hope it's another that convinces you to buy a big bag of chickpea flour.

SERVES 4
40 minutes

INGREDIENTS

2⅓ CUPS (200 G)	Chickpea flour
2 TBSP	Za'atar (or a mix of oregano, basil, thyme and rosemary)
½ TBSP	Flaky sea salt
1 TBSP	Olive oil

FOR THE ROMESCO

¾ CUP (110 G)	Sliced almonds
9 OZ (250 G)	Roasted red peppers from a jar
½ TBSP	Sherry vinegar
1 TSP	Smoked paprika
1	Garlic clove
3 TBSP	Olive oil
—	Salt and freshly ground black pepper

FOR THE BROCCOLI

1 LB (500 G)	Broccolini
1 CUP (150 G)	Edamame beans, fresh or thawed (or peas)
—	Zest and juice of 1 lemon

TIPS
SWAP THE ALMONDS FOR SUNFLOWER SEEDS FOR A CHEAPER, NUT-FREE VERSION. DRIZZLE ANY LEFTOVER ROMESCO OVER VEGETABLES OR BAKED POTATOES, SPREAD ON SANDWICHES OR USE AS A DIP.

1. First, make the batter. Add the chickpea flour to a blender with 2 cups (450 ml) of cold water and blend until smooth. A blender helps to get rid of lumps, but you could also sift the flour into a bowl and whisk in the water until smooth. Add the za'atar and salt and set aside.

2. For the romesco, lightly toast the almonds (save a handful for topping) in a dry pan for 3–4 minutes until golden, stirring often. Drain the peppers and add to a food processor, along with the toasted almonds and the rest of the romesco ingredients. Blend until almost smooth; some texture is nice. Season to taste.

3. Heat the 1 tablespoon of olive oil in a frying pan over medium-high heat. To check if the oil is hot enough, drop a little batter into the pan. If it sizzles, it's ready. Whisk the batter before quickly pouring about a quarter into the hot frying pan. Swirl it around until evenly distributed. Cook for 3–4 minutes on each side until the edges start to curl away from the pan. Gently check that the bottom is cooked by lifting up the edge of the pancake with a spatula—it should be lightly brown on the base. To keep the farinatas warm, place them on a baking sheet, cover with foil and place them in the oven on a low temperature. Repeat with the remaining batter until you have four farinatas.

4. Meanwhile, prepare the broccolini. Remove any tough stems and slice any very thick pieces lengthways down the middle. Add the broccolini and edamame to a large frying pan with a little olive oil, salt and pepper, and cook over medium-high heat for about 8 minutes, until lightly browned and soft. Season well with salt, pepper and the lemon juice.

5. To serve, spread plenty of romesco over each farinata and top with some of the broccolini and edamame. Finish with lemon zest and the remaining toasted almonds.

Cauliflower & Potato Quinoa Wraps with Harissa Yogurt

Turn quinoa into a wrap and fill it with whatever veggies you have. Top with harissa yogurt for a balanced meal full of protein, fiber and flavor.

SERVES 3-4
45 minutes

FOR THE QUINOA WRAPS

1⅓ CUPS (235 G)	Quinoa
½ TSP	Onion powder
½ TSP	Garlic powder
¼ TSP	Salt
½ TSP	Nutritional yeast
–	Oil

FOR THE PICKLED RED ONION (OPTIONAL)

1	Red onion
¼ CUP (60 ML)	Distilled white vinegar
¼ CUP (60 ML)	Apple cider vinegar (or more white vinegar)
1½ TBSP	Sweetener, like agave, maple syrup, sugar
1½ TSP	Salt
¼ TSP	Chile flakes (optional)

FOR THE CAULIFLOWER AND POTATO FILLING

1 LB (500 G)	Cauliflower
14 OZ (400 G)	Potatoes
3 TBSP	Olive oil
1 TSP	Ground cumin
1 TSP	Chile powder
1 TSP	Ground coriander
1 TSP	Smoked paprika
–	Salt and freshly ground black pepper

FOR THE HARISSA YOGURT

2 TSP	Harissa paste
4 TBSP	Plain vegan yogurt (gluten-free and nut-free if needed)

FOR THE LEMON SPINACH

7 OZ (200 G)	Spinach
–	Juice of ½ lemon

1. Rinse the quinoa under cold running water. Place in a heatproof bowl and cover with boiling water. Set aside for 30 minutes.

2. If making the pickled onion, finely slice the onion. In a saucepan, combine ½ cup (120 ml) water with the vinegars, sweetener, salt and chile flakes, if using. Place over medium heat for 3-5 minutes until it starts to boil, then put in a jar with the onion and set aside to pickle. Covered, this will keep in the fridge for up to 2 weeks.

3. Preheat the oven to 470°F (240°C).

4. Cut the cauliflower and potatoes into bite-sized pieces and put them into a large bowl. Drizzle over the olive oil, then scatter in the cumin, chile powder, coriander and smoked paprika. Season with salt and pepper and toss it all together. Spread out on a baking sheet and roast for 25 minutes, or until lightly charred and cooked through, tossing halfway.

5. To make the harissa yogurt, mix the harissa and yogurt in a small bowl and set aside. To make the lemony spinach, add the spinach and a pinch of salt and pepper to a large, dry frying pan over medium heat and cook for a few minutes until wilted. Transfer to a bowl, stir in the lemon juice and season well.

6. When ready to make the wraps, drain the quinoa and rinse it well. Add to a blender with the rest of the wrap ingredients and 1 cup (240 ml) fresh water. Blend until smooth. Heat a little oil in a large, non-stick frying pan over medium-high heat. Pour a small ladle of the quinoa batter into the pan, and use the back of a spoon to spread it out thinly and evenly. Don't worry about perfect edges; all that really matters is that it's thin and evenly spread. Cook for 2 minutes on each side until the wrap is cooked through with brown spots. Repeat with the remaining batter; it should make around 6 wraps.

7. To serve, take a wrap and add a scoop of the cauliflower-and-potato mix. Add some spinach, harissa yogurt and pickled onions, if using. Repeat with the remaining wraps and serve.

● GLUTEN-FREE ● NUT-FREE

Sweet Potatoes with Tahini Butter Chickpeas

This is one of the most popular recipes I've ever shared, so I had to put it in the book too. It's so easy to make and to batch cook, is really filling, has so many layers of flavors and textures and on top of all of that, is healthy too.

SERVES 4
55 minutes

INGREDIENTS

3–4	Sweet potatoes
2 × 14 OZ (400 G)	Cans of chickpeas
5½ OZ (150 G)	Spinach
2	Scallions (optional)
–	Crispy chile oil (nut-free if needed, optional)
3 TBSP	Sesame seeds
–	Salt, freshly ground black pepper and olive oil

FOR THE TAHINI BUTTER

3 TBSP (40 G)	Vegan butter (nut-free if needed), plus extra for the potatoes if you like
3 TBSP	Tahini
½ TBSP	Light soy sauce (or tamari if gluten-free)
½–1 TSP	Maple syrup
1 TBSP	Lemon or lime juice

1. Wash the sweet potatoes well and pierce with a fork all over. Rub them with a little olive oil, salt and pepper. To cook in the oven, preheat the oven to 425°F (220°C) and bake for 40–50 minutes until cooked through. If you prefer, you can air-fry them at 375°F (190°C) for 30–35 minutes, or microwave them on high for 9 minutes in total, turning every 3 minutes.

2. Meanwhile, heat a drizzle of olive oil in a large frying pan over medium heat. Drain the chickpeas and add them to the pan, seasoning well with salt and pepper. Fry for about 8 minutes or until they start to brown and pop. Add the spinach and stir for another few minutes until the spinach has wilted.

3. To make the tahini butter, melt the butter in a small saucepan over low heat, then pour into a small bowl. Add the remaining ingredients, along with 1 tablespoon of warm water, and mix well. It might curdle, but keep mixing. Add a little more water if you need to thin it, as each tahini brand is slightly different.

4. When your potatoes are ready, place them on a plate and slice each one down the middle. If you like, you can add a little vegan butter to the middle of each one at this point. Use a fork to mash the potatoes flat and season them with salt and pepper. Finely slice the scallions, if using.

5. Top the potatoes with the chickpea and spinach mixture, then drizzle plenty of tahini butter over the top. Finish with some crispy chile oil, if using, then scatter over the sesame seeds and finely sliced scallions, if using.

● GLUTEN-FREE ● NUT-FREE

Whipped Pea, Artichoke & Za'atar with New Potatoes

This whipped pea and artichoke combination makes a great base for the warm potato salad. Another protein-packed, balanced meal that's great for meal prep.

SERVES 2–4
30 minutes

INGREDIENTS

1 LB 9 OZ (700 G)	New potatoes
5½ OZ (150 G)	Asparagus spears
3½ OZ (100 G)	Jarred marinated artichokes
1 OZ (35 G)	Arugula
¾ CUP (100 G)	Frozen peas, defrosted
1 TSP	Dijon mustard
–	Juice of ½ lemon
1 TBSP	Olive oil, plus extra for drizzling
2 TBSP	Za'atar
2 TBSP	Toasted sesame seeds (optional)
8–12	Mint leaves
3½ OZ (100 G)	Vegan feta (gluten-free and nut-free, if needed) or tofu—see Tip
–	Salt and freshly ground black pepper

FOR THE WHIPPED PEA & ARTICHOKE PURÉE

¾ CUP (300 G)	Frozen peas, defrosted
3½ OZ (100 G)	Jarred marinated artichokes, plus 2–3 tbsp of their oil
3 TBSP	Lemon juice
1 TSP	Dijon mustard

TIP
IF USING TOFU IN PLACE OF VEGAN FETA, CRUMBLE A HANDFUL INTO A BOWL AND SQUEEZE OVER SOME LEMON JUICE, PLENTY OF SALT AND NUTRITIONAL YEAST. MIX WELL AND MARINATE UNTIL YOU ARE READY TO SERVE.

1. Bring a large pot of salted water to a boil. Add the potatoes and boil for around 15 minutes, or until just cooked through. Take care not to overcook; they should be firm but just soft enough to poke your fork through without resistance.

2. While the potatoes are cooking, add the asparagus spears to the pot for 2 minutes, then remove them with tongs and place them in a colander. Rinse under cold running water to stop them cooking, then set aside.

3. When the potatoes are done, drain them and set them aside in a colander to steam dry.

4. To make the whipped pea and artichoke purée, blend all the ingredients in a small food processor (which will give you a chunky texture) or a blender (for a smooth texture). Season to taste with plenty of salt and pepper.

5. Cut the potatoes into bite-sized pieces. Cut the asparagus spears into 1 in (3 cm) pieces. Thinly slice the artichoke pieces.

6. Combine the potatoes, asparagus, artichokes, arugula and peas in a large bowl. Add the Dijon mustard, lemon juice and olive oil. Toss to combine, and season well to taste.

7. To assemble, spoon plenty of the whipped pea mixture onto a plate. Top with the potatoes and vegetables, then drizzle with a little more olive oil, and sprinkle over the za'atar and sesame seeds, if using. Tear over the mint leaves and crumble on the vegan feta or tofu, then serve.

● GLUTEN-FREE   ● NUT-FREE

Harissa Tomato Couscous

Couscous is something I always have on hand as it takes just 5 minutes to prepare, without any actual cooking. It's a really versatile base, and I love these blistered harissa tomatoes as a topping. Serve as part of a spread or with some tofu, beans or lentils to make a complete meal.

SERVES 2 AS A MAIN, 4 AS A SIDE
30 minutes

INGREDIENTS

1⅓ CUPS (250 G)	Couscous
2 TBSP	Olive oil, plus extra to serve (optional)
¼ CUP (20 G)	Sliced almonds
–	Handful of fresh herbs (parsley, mint and basil would all be great here)
–	Salt and freshly ground black pepper

FOR THE HARISSA TOMATOES

2 TBSP	Olive oil
5½ CUPS (800 G)	Cherry tomatoes
1–2 TBSP	Harissa paste

1. Place the couscous in a medium-sized heatproof bowl. Drizzle over the olive oil, then season with ¾ teaspoon of salt and plenty of pepper and stir well. Pour over 1⅔ cups (400 ml) of boiling water and stir, then leave to absorb for 20 minutes, covering the bowl with foil or a plate.

2. To make the harissa tomatoes, heat the olive oil in a large frying pan over medium heat. Pour in about half the tomatoes and season with salt and pepper. Cook for 5–8 minutes until softened, stirring often, then pour in the rest of the tomatoes and cook for another 4–5 minutes. You want half the tomatoes to be completely broken down into a sauce and half to be intact but softened. Add the harissa and stir through. Taste and adjust the seasoning.

3. Meanwhile, lightly toast the sliced almonds in a dry frying pan over medium heat for a few minutes until evenly golden, stirring often to make sure they don't burn.

4. Finely chop your herbs.

5. When your tomatoes and couscous are ready, it's time to combine them. Reserve a big ladleful of tomatoes for the topping, then stir the rest of them through the couscous until evenly coated.

6. To serve, tip the red couscous onto a large platter and top with the remaining harissa tomatoes, followed by the toasted almonds and fresh herbs. Finish with a final drizzle of olive oil, if you like.

Cozy Bowls · Cozy Bowls

Cozy Bowls · Cozy Bowls

When my body is craving something comforting, warm, filling and rich, I need a big bowl of something cozy. That feeling is really indulged in this chapter. Creamy pastas, warming soups and slurpy, saucy noodles are what I think of when I'm in that mood, and since these are my favorite foods, this chapter is my favorite in the book. While everything here feels indulgent, they are also secretly healthy, nutritious and nourishing.

Balsamic Tomato Macaroni with Olive Pangrattato

This dish is unbelievably tasty and couldn't be simpler to make. The tomatoes, shallots and garlic melt together in olive oil to make the creamy, rich sauce. The olive pangrattato makes it extra special.

SERVES 4
45 minutes

INGREDIENTS

3	Shallots
4–6	Garlic cloves
1 LB (450 G)	Ripe cherry or plum tomatoes
⅓ CUP (75 ML)	Olive oil, plus extra for drizzling
7 OZ (200 G)	Macaroni
3 TBSP	Balsamic vinegar
—	Salt and freshly ground black pepper

FOR THE PANGRATTATO

1	Garlic clove
8–10	Kalamata olives
1	Large slice of sourdough bread (stale works best)
—	Zest of 1 lemon (optional)
1 TBSP	Olive oil

TIP
THE PASTA WILL ABSORB THE SAUCE AS IT SITS, SO ADD A SPLASH OF WATER OR PLANT-BASED MILK TO ANY LEFTOVERS BEFORE REHEATING.

1. Preheat the oven to 425°F (220°C).

2. Peel the shallots and garlic, cut the shallots into eighths and leave the garlic whole. Add these to a small lidded casserole dish or roasting pan—a dish into which everything will fit snugly so that not too much liquid escapes.

3. Add the tomatoes, olive oil and a sprinkle of salt, and shake to coat. Cover with a lid (or cover tightly with foil) and bake for 40 minutes, until everything is very soft. The garlic should melt when pushed with a fork, and the shallots should be completely softened. Everything should be swimming in a pool of garlicky tomato juice.

4. Meanwhile, make the pangrattato. Mince the garlic and finely chop the olives. Process the bread into breadcrumbs in a food processor, then put in a bowl. Add the minced garlic, lemon zest and olive oil, and crumble together with your fingers. Set aside.

5. Heat a large, dry frying pan over medium-high heat. Add the chopped olives and fry for 3–4 minutes, stirring often, until they start to get crispy. Add the breadcrumbs and cook for 3–4 minutes until golden and fragrant. Taste before you season as the olives can be salty. Remove from the pan and set aside.

6. Cook your pasta in a large saucepan of salted boiling water until al dente (1 minute less than the package instructions). Drain and set aside, drizzling with a little olive oil to prevent from sticking.

7. When the tomatoes are ready, remove about a third of them and set aside. Blend the remaining, juice and all, with a stick blender or in a blender, until smooth or almost smooth.

8. Stir the cooked pasta into the sauce. Add the balsamic vinegar and season well with salt and pepper. Ladle the pasta into bowls and top with the reserved tomatoes and olive pangrattato.

● NUT-FREE

Broccoli Pesto Pasta

If you ever have some broccoli that's looking a bit sad and wilted in the back of the fridge, make this pasta. The whole thing is used here—broccoli stalk is perfectly edible and delicious, but often gets wasted.

SERVES 2
25 minutes

INGREDIENTS

7 OZ (200 G)	Spaghetti
3 TBSP	Olive oil, plus extra for drizzling
4–6	Garlic cloves
½ CUP (20 G)	Basil leaves, plus extra for garnish
3 TBSP	Pine nuts, plus extra for garnish (see Tip)
1	Broccoli
2 TBSP	Nutritional yeast
–	Salt

TIP
IF YOU LIKE, YOU CAN SWAP THE PINE NUTS FOR SUNFLOWER SEEDS OR ANY NUT (IF NOT NECESSARY TO BE NUT-FREE).

1. Bring a large pot of salted water to a boil. Add the spaghetti and cook according to the package instructions. Reserve a cup of the pasta water, then drain the pasta and set aside, drizzling it with a little olive oil to stop it sticking.

2. Meanwhile, mince or grate the garlic. Using a food processor or a mortar and pestle, pulse or pound the basil, garlic and pine nuts with a pinch of salt until just pulverized. You want to keep some of the pine nuts whole.

3. Using the largest side of a box grater, grate the whole head of broccoli, stalk and all, leaving only the very tough end.

4. Heat the olive oil in a large frying pan over medium-high heat. Add the grated broccoli and stir-fry for about 8 minutes until it's starting to char.

5. Add the basil mixture to the pan and cook for 2–3 minutes.

6. Tip the spaghetti into the pan and gently stir to coat it in the broccoli pesto. Add a splash or two of the reserved pasta water, and drizzle with plenty of olive oil.

7. Divide the pasta between bowls and sprinkle over the nutritional yeast, extra pine nuts and a few basil leaves to serve.

● NUT-FREE

Sun-Dried Tomato, Chile & Basil Butter Bean Pasta

Often the simplest options are the most effective, and blending butter beans into a creamy sauce is one of my top tips for people trying to eat more plant-based meals. It's accessible, fast, easy, versatile and super healthy. This is one of three blended butter bean pasta sauces in this book—see pages 115 and 116 if you fancy trying one of the others.

SERVES 2
15 minutes

INGREDIENTS

7 OZ (200 G)	Pasta (I used mafalde)
2 TSP	Harissa paste (optional)
–	Juice of ½ lemon
–	Salt and freshly ground black pepper

FOR THE SAUCE

14 OZ (400 G)	Can of butter beans
2 OZ (60 G)	Sun-dried tomatoes
10	Big basil leaves
½–2	Red chiles (depending on how much spice you like)
2 TBSP	Nutritional yeast
2 TBSP	Olive oil, plus extra to serve

TIP

IF YOU HAVE ANY LEFTOVERS, ADD A SPLASH OF WATER BEFORE REHEATING TO HELP LOOSEN THE SAUCE.

1. Empty the can of butter beans into a blender, along with the liquid. Add the other sauce ingredients and blend until smooth.

2. Bring a large pot of salted water to a boil. Add the pasta and cook for 2 minutes less than the package instructions, to get it nice and al dente. Reserve a cupful of the pasta water, then drain the pasta. Return the pasta to the pot and pour over the sauce. Add a good splash of the reserved pasta water and stir to combine and heat through. Taste and season well with salt and pepper.

3. Spoon the pasta into bowls and drizzle over some olive oil and harissa, if using. Finish with a squeeze of lemon and serve.

● NUT-FREE

Greens & Herbs Butter Bean Pasta

The second of my butter bean pasta sauces (see pages 112 and 116 for the others) is a versatile one, allowing you to use up any greens and herbs that might be wilting in your fridge. The flavor is propped up with a few condiments in the sauce, but what really makes this shine is a drizzle of tahini, which gives a smooth, nutty creaminess that is balanced out by a pop of sweet, slightly sour pomegranate molasses.

SERVES 2
15 minutes

INGREDIENTS

7 OZ (200 G)	Pasta (I used orecchiette)
1 TBSP	Tahini
1 TSP	Pomegranate molasses (optional)
—	Juice of ½ lemon
—	Salt and freshly ground black pepper

FOR THE SAUCE

3 TBSP	Raw sunflower seeds (or cashews if not nut-free), plus extra to serve
14 OZ (400 G)	Can of butter beans
½ TSP	Wholegrain mustard
½ TSP	Garlic powder
1¾ OZ (50 G)	Spinach
½ CUP (20 G)	Basil
10 SPRIGS	Flat-leaf parsley
3 TBSP	Nutritional yeast
2 TBSP	Olive oil, plus extra for drizzling

TIP

IF YOU HAVE ANY LEFTOVERS, ADD A SPLASH OF WATER BEFORE REHEATING TO LOOSEN THE SAUCE. YOU COULD ALSO USE IT AS A DIP OR SPREAD IT ON TOAST.

1. Begin by making the sauce. Lightly toast the sunflower seeds (or cashews) in a dry frying pan over medium heat for 2–3 minutes until golden.

2. Empty the can of butter beans into a blender, along with all its liquid. Add the sunflower seeds and all the other sauce ingredients, and blend until smooth. Set aside.

3. Bring a large pot of salted water to a boil. Add the pasta and cook for 2 minutes less than the package instructions, to get it nice and al dente. Reserve a cupful of the pasta water, then drain the pasta. Return the pasta to the pot and pour in the sauce. Add a good splash of the reserved pasta water and stir to combine and heat through. Taste and season well with salt and pepper.

4. Spoon the pasta into bowls and drizzle over some olive oil, along with the tahini and a few dashes of pomegranate molasses, if using. Finish with the extra sunflower seeds and a squeeze of lemon and serve.

● NUT-FREE

Al Limone Butter Bean Pasta

The third of my butter bean pasta sauces (see pages 112 and 115 for the others) is the simplest, and I hope it encourages you to experiment with your own flavor combinations, knowing that there is beauty in simplicity.

SERVES 2
15 minutes

INGREDIENTS

14 OZ (400 G)	Can of butter beans
—	Zest and juice of 1 lemon
1 TBSP	Tahini
1½ TBSP	Olive oil, plus extra to serve
2–3 TBSP	Nutritional yeast
7 OZ (200 G)	Pasta (I used fusilli lunghi)
½ TBSP	Chile flakes (optional)
—	Salt and freshly ground black pepper

TIP
THIS PASTA IS BEST SERVED STRAIGHT AWAY, BUT ADD A SPLASH OF WATER TO ANY LEFTOVERS BEFORE HEATING TO LOOSEN UP THE SAUCE.

1. Drain the butter beans and save the liquid (aquafaba). Measure out a scant ½ cup (100 ml) of the aquafaba and add it to a high-speed blender, along with the butter beans, lemon juice, tahini, olive oil and 2 tablespoons of the nutritional yeast. Season with salt and pepper and blend until smooth. Taste and add more nutritional yeast or salt and pepper, if you like.

2. Bring a large pot of salted water to a boil. Add the pasta and cook for 2 minutes less than the package instructions, to get it nice and al dente. Reserve a cupful of the pasta water, then drain the pasta.

3. Return the pasta to the pot and add the lemony sauce, along with ½ cup (120 ml) of the reserved pasta water. Stir to combine into a silky sauce. Taste and adjust seasonings or add more pasta water as needed. This sauce is great with plenty of pepper, more than you would usually use.

4. Divide between bowls and finish with the lemon zest, a drizzle of olive oil, a scattering of chile flakes, if using, another sprinkle of nutritional yeast and more pepper, if you like.

● NUT-FREE ● ALLIUM-FREE

Coconut Curried Lentil Dal

There are many iterations of dal, a much-loved South Asian dish. This is a creamy version made with puy lentils, which are my favorite as they keep their shape and bite when cooked.

SERVES 4–6

1 hour

INGREDIENTS

2	Onions
6–8	Garlic cloves
¼ CUP (50 G)	Fresh root ginger
2¼ CUPS (450 G)	Puy lentils
3 TBSP	Coconut oil or olive oil
4 TSP	Mustard seeds
4 TSP	Ground turmeric
2 TSP	Ground coriander
2 TSP	Ground cumin
1 TSP	Ground fennel (optional)
1–2 TSP	Chile flakes, plus extra to serve (optional)
2 × 14 OZ (400 ML)	Cans coconut milk (preferably full-fat)
4 OZ (120 G)	Spinach
3 TBSP	Coconut yogurt, plus extra to serve
—	Juice of 1 lime, plus wedges to serve
—	Salt and freshly ground black pepper

1. Finely chop the onions and garlic. Grate the ginger (no need to peel it, just give it a good scrub). Rinse the lentils and pick out any stones.

2. Heat the oil in a large pot over medium-high heat. Add the onion, garlic and 1 teaspoon of salt. When it starts to sizzle, cover the pot, reduce the heat to low, and cook, stirring every so often, for 7–8 minutes until the onion has softened and turned translucent.

3. Add the ginger, mustard seeds, turmeric, coriander, cumin, fennel, if using, and chile flakes. Cook, stirring often, for about 1 minute until fragrant. Add 6⅓ cups (1.5 liters) of water, along with the coconut milk, lentils, and another 1 teaspoon of salt. Bring to a boil then reduce the heat to low. Cover and simmer, stirring a few times, for 40–50 minutes until the lentils are cooked through.

4. Stir in the spinach and increase the heat slightly to bring it back up to a simmer. Taste and season with salt and pepper. Add the coconut yogurt and lime juice and stir through.

5. Ladle the dal into bowls and finish with a sprinkle of chile flakes, if you like. Serve with a couple more spoonfuls of yogurt and lime wedges for squeezing.

● GLUTEN-FREE ● NUT-FREE

Butter Beans with Sticky Soy Portobellos & Thai Basil Pesto

In this recipe, the punchy flavors of the Thai basil pesto and sticky soy marinade are mellowed out by the creamy butter bean base. If you can't find Thai basil, regular basil will do just fine.

SERVES 2
35 minutes

FOR THE MUSHROOMS

2–4	Garlic cloves (to taste)
2 TBSP	Olive oil, plus more for drizzling
1 TBSP	Light soy sauce
1 TSP	Balsamic vinegar
½ TSP	Maple syrup or brown sugar
4	Portobello mushrooms

FOR THE BUTTER BEANS

1–2	Garlic cloves
28 OZ (800 G)	Jar of butter beans (or 2 × 14 oz/ 400 g cans)
2 OZ (60 G)	Baby spinach
2 HEAPED TBSP	Vegan cream cheese
1–2 TBSP	Plant-based milk
—	Salt and freshly ground black pepper

FOR THE THAI BASIL PESTO

¼ CUP (10 G)	Thai basil leaves
¼ CUP (5 G)	Cilantro leaves
1 TBSP (5 G)	Mint leaves
—	Juice of 1 lime
1½ TBSP	Peanuts, plus extra to serve
¼–½	Thai red chile, or 1 tsp Chile flakes (optional)
¼ TSP	Sugar
1½ TSP	Light soy sauce
3 TBSP	Sunflower oil

1. Preheat the oven to 410°F (210°C).

2. Begin by preparing the mushrooms. Mince the garlic, then add it to a bowl with the olive oil, soy sauce, balsamic vinegar and maple syrup, and whisk to combine.

3. Add the mushrooms to the bowl and stir to coat well with the marinade. Tip the whole mushrooms into a baking dish, arranging them gills-side up, and pour any remaining marinade over. Roast for around 20 minutes, or until the mushrooms are cooked through (bigger ones will take longer).

4. Meanwhile, to make the pesto, combine all the ingredients in a small food processor and pulse into a pesto-like consistency.

5. Next, make the creamy butter beans. Mince the garlic and add it to a pot with a drizzle of olive oil, over low-medium heat. Let it sweat for a few minutes, then add the butter beans, along with their liquid. Stir in the spinach and cook for around 5 minutes until soft. Canned beans tend to be harder than jarred, so they will need a little longer. Add the vegan cream cheese and stir through. Season to taste and add the plant-based milk if needed; you want a nice, creamy sauce.

6. When you're ready to serve, spoon the butter beans into bowls. Slice the mushrooms and place them on top of the butter beans. Add a generous spoonful of pesto and finish with a few extra peanuts, if you like, and a drizzle of olive oil.

Chickpea & Blistered Tomato Stew

This is perfect alone as a speedy lunch, or it can be served with crusty bread or your favorite grain for something more substantial. It is such a versatile recipe; try some different beans, vegetables and condiments depending on what you have on hand.

SERVES 1-2
15 minutes

INGREDIENTS

3-4	Garlic cloves
2 TBSP	Olive oil, plus extra for drizzling
2⅔ CUPS (400 G)	Cherry tomatoes
14 OZ (400 G)	Can of chickpeas (or cannellini or butter beans)
2 TBSP	Nutritional yeast
1¾ OZ (50 G)	Baby spinach
1 TBSP	Pine nuts
2 TBSP	Tahini (see Tip)
–	Zest and juice of ½ lemon
–	Salt and black pepper
–	Chopped fresh herbs, to garnish (basil, parsley or dill work)

TO SERVE (OPTIONAL)

–	Sourdough or focaccia
–	Chile flakes
–	Dukkah
–	Sun-dried tomatoes

TIP

YOU HAVE A FEW OPTIONS TO MAKE THIS CREAMY, DEPENDING ON WHAT YOU LIKE AND WHAT YOU HAVE. INSTEAD OF TAHINI, YOU CAN USE A TABLESPOON OF VEGAN CREAM CHEESE (A HERBY ONE WOULD BE GREAT), HUMMUS, CASHEW OR COCONUT CREAM, OR 2 TABLESPOONS OF PLANT-BASED MILK. YOU COULD ALSO BLEND A COUPLE OF TABLESPOONS OF THE CHICKPEAS AND STIR THEM THROUGH.

1. Finely mince the garlic.

2. Heat the olive oil in a medium-sized pot over medium heat. Once hot, add the tomatoes (take care as they might spit when they hit the oil). Sprinkle with a little salt and let them cook for 3–5 minutes until they start to blister. Add the garlic and cook for 1 minute, then add the chickpeas, along with all the liquid from the can.

3. Cook for 5–6 minutes until the liquid has thickened, lightly crushing the tomatoes so they release their juices. Try not to reduce all the liquid, but if you do, just add a splash of water. Add the nutritional yeast and stir in the spinach until wilted.

4. Meanwhile, lightly toast the pine nuts in a hot, dry frying pan for 2–3 minutes until golden.

5. When the chickpeas are cooked, add the tahini (or your chosen creamy ingredient) and season well with plenty of salt and pepper. Use your spoon to mash some of the chickpeas to get a creamy texture.

6. Spoon the stew into a bowl or two, drizzle over some olive oil, top with some lemon zest and a good squeeze of lemon, and finish with the chopped herbs, your toasted pine nuts and any of the optional extras.

Leek & Miso Orzo with Preserved Lemon Chile Jam

This one surprised me when I first made it, and it has surprised everyone who's tried it since, because of its perfectly balanced flavors. The unassuming, creamy, umami-packed pasta dish is elevated even further with the preserved lemon chile jam. It's one I keep coming back to again and again.

SERVES 4
35 minutes

INGREDIENTS

3	Leeks
3–4	Garlic cloves
2 TBSP	Vegan butter (nut-free if needed)
2 TBSP	Olive oil
2¼ CUPS (500 G)	Orzo
2	Vegetable stock cubes
⅔ CUP (160 ML)	Unsweetened plant-based milk (nut-free if needed)
4 TSP	Miso paste
2 TBSP	Nutritional yeast (optional)
4 TBSP	Tahini (optional)
—	Salt and freshly ground black pepper

FOR THE PRESERVED LEMON CHILE JAM

4 OZ (120 G)	Preserved lemon
4 TBSP	Olive oil
2 TSP	Tomato paste
2 TSP	Chile flakes
2½ TSP	Smoked paprika

TIPS
IF YOU DON'T HAVE VEGAN BUTTER, JUST REPLACE WITH MORE OLIVE OIL.

ANY LEFTOVER PRESERVED LEMON JAM CAN BE STORED IN AN AIRTIGHT CONTAINER IN THE FRIDGE FOR UP TO 5 DAYS.

1. Finely slice the leeks and mince the garlic.

2. Melt the butter and oil in a large pot over low-medium heat. Add the leeks and garlic and sweat for 10–15 minutes, then add the orzo to the pot. Stir to coat it in butter and oil and lightly toast.

3. In a jug, dissolve the stock cubes in 4 cups (1 liter) of boiling water, then pour this into the pot. Increase the heat to high and bring to a boil, then reduce the heat to low and simmer, with the lid slightly ajar to allow some steam out. Cook for about 15 minutes, stirring often. Add a little more water if needed.

4. Warm the plant-based milk in a small saucepan over low heat, then whisk through the miso. Pour the miso and milk mixture over the orzo and stir. Add the nutritional yeast, if using, and season to taste.

5. Meanwhile, make the jam. Deseed and finely chop the preserved lemon. Add the olive oil, preserved lemon, tomato paste, chile flakes and smoked paprika to a small frying pan or saucepan. Cook for 3–4 minutes on low heat until the mixture has emulsified and combined into a jammy texture surrounded by oil.

6. To serve, spoon the orzo into bowls, then top with a few teaspoons of preserved lemon jam and a drizzle of tahini, if using.

Lemony Bean Stew

This is inspired by Greek fasolada. There are many iterations of Greek bean stews and they usually start with dried beans. I've cut some corners here to make it a speedy weeknight meal. It's cozy, hearty and packed full of flavor and nutrients.

SERVES 4–6
35 minutes

INGREDIENTS

2	Celery sticks
3–5	Garlic cloves
1	Onion
2	Carrots
¾ CUP (10 G)	Fresh dill (or 1 tsp dried dill), plus extra to serve
2 × 14 OZ (400 G)	Cans of cannellini beans (or any other white bean)
½ CUP (100 G)	Jasmine rice
1	Vegetable stock cube (gluten-free if needed)
3 TBSP	Tahini
2 TBSP	Nutritional yeast (optional)
–	Zest and juice of 2–3 lemons
–	Salt, freshly ground black pepper and olive oil

1. Finely dice the celery. Peel and finely chop the garlic and onion. Scrub the carrots clean and halve lengthways, then finely slice. Finely chop the dill.

2. Heat a good glug of olive oil in a large pot over medium heat and add the celery, carrot, garlic and onion. Season with salt and pepper and cook for about 10 minutes until softened but not brown, stirring occasionally.

3. Meanwhile, drain and rinse the beans.

4. Add the rice to the pot and cook for 1 minute, stirring. Now pour in 4¼ cups (1 liter) of water, along with the stock cube, dill and beans, then bring to a boil. Reduce the heat to low and cover with the lid slightly ajar to let some steam out. Simmer for about 15 minutes, or until the rice is cooked and the beans are very tender.

5. Stir in the tahini and nutritional yeast, if using. Add the juice of 2 lemons and taste, then decide if you want to add more (I use the juice of 3 lemons, but I love a strong lemon flavor!). Stir well and add an extra splash of water if needed; the soup will thicken as it cools.

6. Taste and adjust the seasonings, adding about twice as much black pepper as you usually would, as this will really draw out the flavors in the soup.

7. Ladle into bowls and sprinkle the lemon zest over each bowl, along with some extra dill. Top each one with a final drizzle of olive oil, then serve.

Hot & Sticky Stir-Fry with Rice Noodles

This dish is all about the prep. Before you start, have everything ready to throw into the pan and your meal will come together in no time. This take-out style sauce is perfect for using up odd ends of veggies.

SERVES 2
30 minutes

INGREDIENTS

½	Head of broccoli
1	Large bok choi, or a few handfuls of kale or spinach
10 OZ (280 G)	Extra-firm tofu
1 TBSP	Cornstarch
30	Twists of black pepper
2–3 TBSP	Sunflower oil
½ CUP (50 G)	Cashews
7 OZ (200 G)	Flat rice noodles or jasmine rice
3 TBSP	Sesame seeds
–	Handful of Thai basil (or Italian basil)
–	Handful of mint leaves
1	Lime, cut into wedges
–	Salt

FOR THE SAUCE

10	Garlic cloves
4	Scallions
1–3	Red chiles (depending on your heat preference)
1 TBSP	Chile flakes (optional)
4 TBSP	Ketchup
2 TBSP	Dark soy sauce (or tamari if gluten-free)
2 TBSP	Agave or maple syrup
2 TBSP	Sunflower oil

1. To prepare the ingredients for the sauce, mince the garlic cloves and set aside in a small bowl. Thinly slice the scallions and add the whites to the garlic bowl, keeping the green tops aside for later. Finely slice the chile(s) and add to the bowl.

2. In a separate bowl, mix together your chile flakes, if using, ketchup, soy sauce and agave or maple syrup, along with 2 tablespoons of water. Set aside.

3. Now cut the broccoli into bite-sized pieces. Separate the bok choi leaves and halve any large ones lengthways. Pat the tofu dry with a paper towel and crumble it into bite-sized pieces in a bowl. Add the cornstarch and the twists of black pepper and toss to combine.

4. Heat 2 tablespoons of the sunflower oil in a large frying pan or wok over high heat. Add the tofu and fry for 5–6 minutes until starting to crisp up, stirring occasionally. Next, add the broccoli and bok choi, along with another tablespoon of sunflower oil if needed, and fry for another 5 minutes.

5. Empty everything from the pan into a large bowl. Add the cashews to this bowl, too.

6. Return to the sauce. Heat the 2 tablespoons of oil in the now-empty pan over medium heat. Add the chile(s), scallion whites and garlic, and fry for 3 minutes until starting to crisp up, stirring often. Add the ketchup sauce to the pan and stir for about 30 seconds to cook and combine. Now return the vegetables and cashews to the pan and fry for 2 minutes until well coated. Taste and season with salt and pepper.

7. Meanwhile, cook your noodles or rice according to the package instructions. Divide the noodles or rice between two bowls, then top with the stir-fried vegetables. Sprinkle over plenty of sesame seeds and tear over the Thai basil and mint leaves. Serve with lime wedges for squeezing.

Minced Tofu with Herby Cucumber Salad & Sriracha Mayo

There are so many ways to make tofu tasty, but this has to be one of my favorites. Grating it creates a meaty texture which clings to and absorbs all the flavors of the marinade. It's an easy, crispy and versatile way of preparing tofu that also works great on top of noodles.

SERVES 2
30 minutes

FOR THE TOFU

10 OZ (280 G)	Extra-firm tofu
4–5	Scallions
1 TBSP	Tomato paste
½ TSP	Smoked paprika
2 TBSP	Nutritional yeast
1½ TBSP	Light soy sauce
1 TSP	Mild chile powder
1 TBSP	Sesame oil
1 TBSP	Sunflower or olive oil
2 TBSP	Sesame seeds, plus extra to serve
½ TSP	Onion powder (optional)
½ TSP	Garlic powder (optional)
–	Vegetable oil
1 TBSP	Mirin (optional)

FOR THE SALAD

1 OZ (25 G)	Fresh herbs (basil, mint and cilantro are all great)
1	Cucumber
1	Red or green chile
–	Juice of 1 lime
2 TBSP	Sesame oil
–	Salt

FOR THE SRIRACHA MAYO

3 TSP	Vegan mayonnaise
1 TSP	Sriracha

TO SERVE

¾ CUP (150 G)	Jasmine rice

1. Use a box grater to grate the tofu. Tip the grated tofu into a clean tea towel and squeeze out any excess water. Halve the scallions lengthways, then slice each half into 1 in (3 cm) pieces.

2. In a large bowl, whisk the rest of the tofu ingredients (except the scallions, vegetable oil and mirin, if using), then add the tofu. Stir well to combine and set aside to marinate.

3. To make the salad, chop the herbs and add them to a bowl. Halve the cucumber lengthways and scoop out the watery seeds with a spoon, then thinly slice the flesh on the diagonal and add to the bowl. Deseed and finely slice the chile. Add the lime juice and sesame oil, and season with salt. Toss to combine.

4. Rinse the rice thoroughly under cold running water, then tip into a pot. Add 1 cup (240 ml) of water to the pot, then cover with a lid and bring to a boil over high heat. As soon as it's boiling, reduce the heat to medium and cook for 5 minutes, then reduce the heat to low and gently simmer for another 5 minutes. Remove from the heat and leave to stand, with the lid on, for 5 minutes more.

5. Meanwhile, to cook the tofu, heat a drizzle of vegetable oil in a large frying pan over medium-high heat. Add the tofu and fry for about 3–4 minutes until it's starting to crisp up, then add the chopped scallions and mirin and cook for another 3–4 minutes until the onions have softened and the tofu is cooked. It should be crispy with some soft bits.

6. For the sriracha mayo, mix the two ingredients together. Easy.

7. When everything is ready, spoon the rice into bowls and top with the tofu, salad and a big dollop of sriracha mayo. Finish with some more sesame seeds and a squeeze of leftover lime.

● NUT-FREE

Roasted Cauliflower Gnocchi

Cauliflower is a magical ingredient that can morph into a deeply caramelized cream as well as delicious, perfectly cooked bites. This recipe has both, and if you've never tried roasted cauliflower blended into a creamy sauce, you might be surprised at how delicious it is.

SERVES 4
35 minutes

INGREDIENTS

¾ CUP (85 G)	Cashews
1	Cauliflower (about 2 lb 4 oz/1 kg)
1 LB 12 OZ (800 G)	Vegan gnocchi
2 CUPS (500 ML)	Unsweetened plant-based milk
3 TBSP	Nutritional yeast
1½ TSP	White miso paste
1 TSP	Wholegrain mustard
½ TSP	Maple syrup (optional)
1 TBSP	Vegan butter or olive oil
–	Salt, freshly ground black pepper and olive oil
–	Few sprigs of dill or parsley, to serve

TIPS

YOU CAN ENJOY THE CAULIFLOWER LEAVES AS A QUICK SNACK WHILE YOU COOK. SIMPLY REMOVE THE TOUGH SPINE AND DRIZZLE THEM WITH A LITTLE OLIVE OIL, THEN SEASON. ADD SOME CHILE FLAKES IF YOU LIKE. ROAST FOR 10–15 MINUTES UNTIL CRISPY, TOSSING HALFWAY.

ANY LEFTOVER SAUCE CAN BE USED AS A DRESSING FOR VEGETABLES OR GRAINS, OR THINNED DOWN INTO A SOUP.

1. Preheat the oven to 425°F (220°C).

2. Tip the cashews onto a large baking sheet and roast for 5 minutes. Set aside.

3. Chop your cauliflower into bite-sized florets and place in a roasting pan. Drizzle with olive oil and season with salt and pepper, then roast on the top rack of the oven for 20–25 minutes, turning halfway. The cauliflower should be charred in spots and still have a firm bite to it.

4. Meanwhile, cook your gnocchi according to the package instructions. Drain and set aside.

5. Reserve a handful of roasted cauliflower florets and a handful of the cashews for garnish, and add the rest to a high-speed blender. Add the plant-based milk, nutritional yeast, miso, mustard and 1 tablespoon of olive oil. Season with plenty of salt and pepper, and blend until smooth. Taste for seasoning; some cauliflower can be a bit bitter, especially if it's not very fresh, so if this is the case, add a little maple syrup to balance out the bitterness.

6. Melt the butter or heat the olive oil in a large pot over medium heat. Add the drained gnocchi and sauté for a couple of minutes to crisp up the edges a little. Add the sauce to the pot, bit by bit, until you reach your desired creaminess (see Tip). Stir in the reserved cauliflower.

7. Roughly chop the reserved roasted cashews.

8. Spoon the gnocchi into bowls and serve sprinkled with the fresh herbs and reserved cashews.

ALLIUM-FREE

Savory Oats with Soy Butter Shiitake

Treat your oats like a risotto, using them as the base for a quick, fiber-packed dinner. This dish is inspired by congee—a delicious type of savory rice porridge eaten in many Asian countries at different times of the day. Make sure to use thick jumbo oats, as they hold their shape to give a creamy texture that's not gloopy.

SERVES 4
30 minutes

INGREDIENTS

2 CUPS (250 G)	Jumbo oats (gluten-free if needed)
1	Vegetable stock cube (gluten-free if needed)
1 TSP	Vegan butter
2 TSP	Crispy chile oil (optional)
2 TBSP	Sesame seeds and/or roasted peanuts
—	Salt, freshly ground black pepper and olive oil

FOR THE SOY BUTTER MUSHROOMS

7 OZ (200 G)	Mushrooms (I use shiitake)
1	Scallion
1	Garlic clove
1 TBSP	Vegan butter
2 TSP	Light soy sauce (or tamari if gluten-free)

FOR THE MISO PEANUT BUTTER DRIZZLE

2 TBSP	Smooth peanut butter
2 TSP	Miso paste
1 TSP	Light soy sauce (or tamari if gluten-free)
1 TSP	Sesame oil
2 TSP	Maple syrup
—	Squeeze of lemon or lime juice

1. Start by toasting your oats. This is not essential, but it adds an extra layer of flavor. Simply add the oats to a large, dry pot over medium heat and toast for 3–5 minutes, stirring often, until fragrant.

2. Pour 4¼ cups (1 liter) of water into the pot, along with the stock cube. Bring to a boil, then reduce the heat to low and simmer for 5–8 minutes, stirring often. The more you stir, the creamier the oats will become. Add the vegan butter and season with salt and pepper.

3. Remove from the heat and taste the oats to check they are done. They should be creamy, not chalky, not too thick, and with a nice bite to them.

4. Meanwhile, cook the mushrooms. Finely slice the mushrooms and the scallion, setting aside the green parts for garnish. Mince the garlic clove.

5. Heat a splash of olive oil in a frying pan over medium heat. Add the mushrooms, scallion whites, minced garlic and a pinch of salt. Fry for about 5 minutes until the mushrooms have cooked through and caramelized nicely. Add the vegan butter and soy sauce and stir through. As soon as the butter has melted, remove the pan from the heat.

6. To make the drizzle, simply whisk together all the ingredients in a small bowl with 2 tablespoons of hot water until smooth. Taste and add more lemon, maple syrup or soy sauce to taste.

7. When everything is ready, spoon the oats into two bowls and top with the mushrooms, then drizzle over the miso peanut butter sauce and some chile oil, if using. Finish with a scattering of sesame seeds or peanuts and the reserved scallion.

Tomato & Tofu Curry

Inspired by the flavors of a classic Indian tomato curry, this is my speedy, easy version that's packed full of protein.

SERVES 2
30 minutes

INGREDIENTS

1	Onion
4	Garlic cloves
2 TBSP (25 G)	Fresh root ginger
1½ TSP	Ground cumin (or 1 tsp cumin seeds)
3 TBSP	Sliced almonds
12 OZ (350 G)	Firm tofu
2 TBSP	Vegan butter
2 TBSP	Neutral oil, such as sunflower or canola oil
1 TBSP	Tomato paste
¼ TSP	Ground turmeric
½ TSP	Garam masala
1–2 TSP	Chile powder
14 OZ (400 G)	Can of plum tomatoes or chopped tomatoes
¾ CUP (100 G)	Frozen peas
3–5 TBSP	Unsweetened coconut yogurt or soy yogurt
—	Salt and freshly ground black pepper
—	Cooked rice or flatbreads (gluten-free if needed), to serve

1. Finely chop the onion and mince the garlic and ginger. Gently crush the cumin seeds, if using, or leave them whole for a slightly sweet burst of flavor. Lightly toast the sliced almonds in a dry frying pan over medium-low heat for 3–4 minutes until golden, then set aside.

2. Slice the tofu block in half down the thinnest side, so you have two thin blocks. Pat with a clean tea towel to remove as much moisture as possible, then cut the tofu into cubes.

3. Melt the butter in a large saucepan over medium heat. Add the tofu and fry for 5–6 minutes until it's golden on all sides, turning gently. Remove from the pan and set aside on a plate lined with paper towels. Season well with salt and pepper.

4. While the tofu is cooking, heat the oil in a medium-sized saucepan over low-medium heat. Add the onion, ginger and garlic and fry for 5–8 minutes until translucent.

5. Add the tomato paste and spices and fry for another minute, then add the canned tomatoes. Cook for 3–4 minutes until fragrant, then add the peas and 3 tablespoons of the yogurt. Stir to incorporate, then taste and adjust the seasonings as necessary. You may want to add more chile for heat or more yogurt for creaminess.

6. Add the tofu to the pan and mix well.

7. Serve topped with the toasted almonds, with cooked rice or flatbreads on the side.

GLUTEN-FREE

Pulled Eggplant Ragu with Hummus Mashed Potato

The first time I thought of putting hummus in my mashed potatoes, it was a revelation. It adds protein, creaminess and a different layer of flavor, and is a great way to use up leftover hummus. And there's nothing better to pile on to your mash than a rich, saucy ragu.

SERVES 4
1 hour 25 minutes

FOR THE RAGU

1 OZ (30 G)	Dried mushrooms (wild, oyster, porcini or a mix)
3	Medium eggplants
1	Carrot
1	Onion
1	Celery stick
4	Garlic cloves
3 TBSP	Olive oil
3 TBSP	Tomato paste
1 TBSP	Balsamic vinegar
½ CUP (125 ML)	Red wine
1	Vegetable stock cube (gluten-free if needed)
3 TBSP	Nutritional yeast
1⅔ CUPS (400 ML)	Tomato passata or puréed tomatoes
—	Salt and freshly ground black pepper

FOR THE HUMMUS MASH

2¾ LB (1.25 KG)	Potatoes
1⅓ CUPS (350 G)	Hummus (store-bought or homemade)
1 TBSP	Olive oil

FOR THE WALNUT PARM

¼ CUP (35 G)	Walnuts
1 TBSP	Nutritional yeast
¼ TSP	Garlic powder
¼–½ TSP	Flaky sea salt

1. In a bowl, pour 1¼ cups (300 ml) of boiling water over the dried mushrooms, then set aside to soak.

2. Preheat the oven to 410°F (210°C).

3. Pierce the eggplants all over with a fork. Arrange on a baking sheet and roast for 45–55 minutes (depending on their size). Alternatively, you can burn them over a gas burner by placing them over the flame for 15–20 minutes, turning frequently with metal tongs, until they are evenly charred. They are done when the skin is wrinkly and they are very soft, almost collapsing in on themselves.

4. When the eggplants are cooked, set them aside to cool, covered with a plate or lid. Once cool, carefully peel them (the skin should come off very easily), then use your fingers or a fork to pull the flesh into long, thick strips.

5. Meanwhile, peel and finely dice the carrot and onion. Finely dice the celery and mince the garlic. Heat the olive oil in a large pot over medium heat. Add the onion, carrot, garlic and celery and season with plenty of salt and pepper. Sauté for 10–15 minutes until softened but not brown.

6. Add the tomato paste, balsamic vinegar and wine, and let it cook off for a few minutes until the wine has reduced. Then add the mushrooms, along with their soaking water, taking care not to add any grit that may have gathered at the bottom of the bowl. Add the stock cube, nutritional yeast and passata, and stir to combine.

7. Bring to a boil, then reduce the heat to low and simmer, stirring occasionally, for 15–20 minutes. If it's looking dry, add a splash of water.

CONTINUED OVERLEAF

RECIPE CONTINUED

8. Add the eggplants to the sauce and stir gently. Cook for another few minutes to combine the flavors, and season very well with salt and pepper.

9. Meanwhile, bring a large pot of well-salted water to a boil. Peel the potatoes and cut them into chunks. Once the water has come to a boil, add the potatoes and cook for 12–15 minutes or until just cooked. Drain and leave to steam dry for a few minutes in the colander.

10. Return the potatoes to the empty pot. Add the hummus and use a potato masher or a fork to mash them until smooth. Season well with salt and pepper and stir in the olive oil to give it some extra creaminess.

11. To make the walnut parm, lightly toast the walnuts in a dry frying pan over medium heat for 3–5 minutes. Add them to a small blender or finely chop by hand. Process or stir in the rest of the ingredients.

12. To serve, spoon a generous amount of hummus mash into a bowl, then load with the pulled eggplant ragu and top with the walnut parm. Enjoy.

Roasted Chile & Squash Spelt with Smoky Sunflower Seed Crunch

Spelt is an ancient grain that's packed with nutrients and has an earthy, nutty flavor and a firm bite. It's a delicious, healthy substitute for white rice, orzo or risotto rice, and works perfectly here in this creamy, filling dish.

SERVES 4

1 hour

INGREDIENTS

2 CUPS (400 G)	Pearled spelt or barley
1	Vegetable stock cube
1	Butternut squash (about 2 lb 4 oz/1 kg)
1	Red onion
1	Garlic bulb
2	Small chiles (optional)
1 TSP	Smoked paprika
1 TBSP	Tahini
—	Juice of ½ lemon
1–2 CUPS (250–500 G)	Unsweetened plant milk (nut-free if needed)
—	Salt, freshly ground black pepper and olive oil
—	Handful of fresh parsley, to serve (optional)

FOR THE SUNFLOWER SEED CRISP

2 TBSP	Olive oil
4 TBSP	Sunflower seeds
½ TSP	Smoked paprika
—	Juice of ½ lemon
—	Pinch of chile flakes (optional)

TIP

MAKE SURE TO BUY PEARLED SPELT OR BARLEY, AS UNPEARLED WILL TAKE MUCH LONGER TO COOK. PEARLED MEANS THAT THE OUTER LAYER HAS BEEN REMOVED, WHICH REDUCES THE COOKING TIME AND MAKES FOR A SOFTER GRAIN.

1. Rinse the spelt twice and then cover with fresh, cold water. Soak for at least 20 minutes or overnight, then drain.

2. Pour 4¼ cups (1 liter) of fresh water into a large pot and add the stock cube and spelt. Bring to a boil, then reduce the heat to low and simmer for 20 minutes or until cooked through. The spelt should have a firm bite but not be too hard or too soft. Drain well and return it to the pot.

3. Preheat the oven to 400°F (200°C) and line a baking sheet with parchment paper.

4. Peel the squash and chop into ½ in (1 cm) cubes. Set the skin and seeds aside to use in stock or you can roast them for a snack (see Note overleaf).

5. Thickly slice the onion. Cut the top off the garlic bulb. If using, halve the chiles lengthways and deseed.

6. Spread out the squash, chiles, onion and garlic on the prepared baking sheet. Drizzle with olive oil, and season with salt, pepper and paprika. Roast for 30–35 minutes or until soft and starting to brown, tossing halfway, then allow to cool slightly.

7. When cool enough to handle, squeeze the garlic cloves out of the skin and add to a blender. Reserve a couple of handfuls of squash cubes for garnish, then tip the rest of the contents of the baking sheet into the blender. Add the tahini, lemon juice, plant milk and 2 tablespoons of olive oil and blend until smooth. Taste and season well with salt and pepper.

CONTINUED OVERLEAF

● NUT-FREE

RECIPE CONTINUED

8   Slowly add half the sauce into the pot with the spelt and stir, then keep adding more as you like, depending on how creamy you want your dish to be. (You may have some sauce leftover, which can be stored for up to 3 days in the fridge and served with roasted vegetables or grains.) Add the reserved squash cubes too. Stir and heat gently, adding a little more plant milk if needed. Taste and season again.

9   To make the crispy sunflower seeds, heat the olive oil in a small frying pan over medium heat. Add the sunflower seeds and fry for 3–5 minutes until golden brown, stirring often. Remove from the heat and transfer to a bowl, then stir in the paprika, lemon juice and chile flakes, if using. Season with salt and pepper. Add some extra olive oil if it has become too dry.

10 Divide the spelt between bowls and spoon over the sunflower seeds. Top with fresh herbs, if using, then serve.

NOTE

YOU CAN USE THE SQUASH SKIN AND SEEDS TO MAKE A TASTY SNACK.

FOR CRISPY SQUASH SKIN, SEASON THE SKINS WITH SALT AND PEPPER AND DRIZZLE WITH A LITTLE OLIVE OIL. ROAST IN THE OVEN FOR 8-12 MINUTES AT 425°F (220°C) OR UNTIL GOLDEN BROWN. ALTERNATIVELY, AIR-FRY FOR 8 MINUTES AT 350°F (180°C).

FOR CRISPY SQUASH SEEDS, PLACE THE SEEDS IN A SMALL BOWL OF WATER: THIS MAKES IT EASIER TO REMOVE THE SQUASH MEMBRANE. CLEAN THE SEEDS AS BEST YOU CAN, THEN DRAIN. SPREAD THEM OUT ON A SMALL BAKING SHEET WITH A TINY DRIZZLE OF OLIVE OIL, THEN SEASON WITH SMOKED PAPRIKA, SALT AND PEPPER. ROAST FOR 8 MINUTES AT 425°F (220°C), TOSSING HALFWAY.

The New Cream of Mushroom Soup

This is my version of a much-loved classic. It's just as comforting but far more nourishing, as it's made with silken tofu, which gives a smooth creaminess. Using tofu as a cream is my favorite way to sneak in some extra protein.

SERVES 4

1 hour

INGREDIENTS

1	Vegetable stock cube (gluten-free if needed)
¾ OZ (20 G)	Dried mixed mushrooms (such as porcini, oyster and wild mushrooms)
1	Onion
4–6	Garlic cloves
1 LB (500 G)	Button mushrooms
1 TBSP	Olive oil, plus extra for drizzling
2 TBSP	Vegan butter (nut-free if needed)
⅓ CUP (75 ML)	White wine (optional)
10½ OZ (300 G)	Silken tofu
1 TBSP	White miso paste
1 TBSP	Soy sauce (or tamari if gluten-free)
—	Salt and freshly ground black pepper
—	Handful of chives, to garnish

NOTE

IF YOU HAVE ANY VEGAN CREAM CHEESE (GLUTEN-FREE AND NUT-FREE IF NEEDED) KICKING AROUND, FEEL FREE TO STIR IN A TABLESPOON AT THE END FOR SOME EXTRA CREAMINESS AND FLAVOR.

1. In a large measuring jug or heatproof bowl, dissolve the stock cube in 3 cups (700 ml) of boiling water. Once it's fully dissolved, add the dried mushrooms. Set aside.

2. Finely dice the onion and finely chop the garlic. Slice the button mushrooms.

3. Heat the olive oil in a medium-sized pot over medium heat. Add the onion and season with some salt and pepper. Sauté for about 5 minutes until translucent, then add the garlic and sauté for another 2 minutes.

4. Add the vegan butter to the pot and, once it has melted, add the button mushrooms. Season generously with salt and pepper and increase the heat to high. Cook for 12–15 minutes, or until the mushrooms have released most of their liquid and are starting to char, stirring occasionally. The longer you cook the mushrooms here, the more depth of flavor they will have.

5. Add the white wine, if using, and allow it to cook off completely for a few minutes, stirring a few times to deglaze the bottom of the pan. Make sure the smell of alcohol has completely gone.

6. Pour in the mushroom stock, along with the soaked mushrooms, leaving behind any grit settled at the bottom of the jug. Stir and bring to a boil, then reduce the heat to low and simmer for 10 minutes, covered.

7. Remove 3–4 tablespoons of the mushrooms and set aside for the topping. Add the silken tofu, miso, and soy sauce to the pot. Blend with a stick blender or pour into a high-speed blender and blend until completely smooth.

8. Bring the soup back to a gentle simmer for about 5 minutes to thicken slightly. You can leave it to simmer for longer if you prefer a thicker soup. Taste and adjust the seasonings to taste.

9. Ladle into bowls and drizzle with olive oil. Top with the reserved mushrooms, black pepper, and the chopped chives.

Green Coconut Noodle Soup

This vibrant green soup is one of my all-time favorites because it's velvety smooth, full of flavors and textures, and is so simple to put together. Feel free to try it with different toppings, like baby corn or crispy tofu.

SERVES 2
30 minutes

INGREDIENTS

2	Shallots
3	Garlic cloves
1–2	Red chiles
3 TBSP (40 G)	Fresh root ginger
2 TBSP	Coconut oil (or sunflower oil)
7 OZ (200 G)	Shiitake mushrooms
1	Vegetable stock cube (gluten-free if needed)
3 TBSP	White miso paste
3 TBSP	Light soy sauce (or tamari if gluten-free), plus a splash
1 BUNCH (70 G)	Cilantro
14 OZ (400 ML)	Can of coconut milk
7 OZ (200 G)	Broccoli or tenderstem broccoli
5½ OZ (150 G)	Flat rice noodles
–	Juice of 2 limes
–	Crispy chile oil (optional, check the label if gluten-free)
–	Salt

1. Finely chop the shallots, garlic, chile(s) and ginger. Reserve a few chile slices for garnish.

2. Melt 1 tablespoon of the coconut oil in a pot over low heat. Add the shallots, garlic, chile and ginger, and season with salt. Sauté for 5–6 minutes until soft but not browned.

3. Meanwhile, remove the stems from the shiitake mushrooms. Finely chop the stems and set the tops aside for now. Add the chopped stems to the pot with the shallots, and sauté for a few minutes more. Pour 4¼ cups (1 liter) of water into the pot and add the stock cube.

4. Remove a ladleful of broth and pour it into a small bowl. Add the miso to the bowl and whisk well until fully incorporated. Pour this back into the pot, along with the soy sauce, and stir. Leave to simmer on low while you complete the next steps.

5. Remove the tough stems from the cilantro and set aside a few leaves for garnish. Add the rest to a blender, along with the coconut milk, and blend until smooth.

6. Thinly slice the reserved shiitake tops and chop the broccoli into small pieces. Heat the remaining tablespoon of coconut oil in a frying pan over medium heat. Add the shiitake and broccoli and sauté for 8–12 minutes until browned. Add a splash of soy sauce at the end, and set aside.

7. Cook the noodles according to the package instructions.

8. Add the coconut and cilantro mixture to the broth and warm through, then remove from the heat (the cilantro will start to turn very dark in color if it's heated for too long).

9. To serve, add the noodle broth to a bowl and top with the shiitakes and broccoli. Finish with a good squeeze of lime juice, the reserved cilantro leaves and a drizzle of chile oil, if you like.

● GLUTEN-FREE   ● NUT-FREE

Creamy Celeriac & Almond Soup with Preserved Lemon Gremolata

When I first started developing this recipe, it was a roasted celeriac and hazelnut butter sauce for gnocchi. If that inspires you, just reduce the amount of liquid to make this creamy, earthy, nutty sauce for any pasta.

SERVES 2-4
45 minutes

INGREDIENTS

2 LB 4 OZ (1 KG)	Celeriac (celery root)
2	Garlic cloves
2	Shallots
3 TBSP	Vegan butter or olive oil
1	Vegetable stock cube (gluten-free if needed)
14 OZ (400 G)	Can of cannellini beans
12–18	Thyme sprigs
1⅔ CUPS (400 ML)	Unsweetened plant-based milk (gluten-free if needed)
2–3 TBSP	Almond butter
2 TBSP	Vegan cream cheese (optional, gluten-free if needed)
—	Salt and freshly ground black pepper
—	Chile flakes, to garnish (optional)

FOR THE ALMOND GREMOLATA

¼ CUP (25 G)	Sliced almonds
¾ OZ (20 G)	Preserved lemon (or 1 tbsp lemon juice + ½ tsp lemon zest)
¼ CUP (15 G)	Flat-leaf parsley
3½ TBSP	Olive oil

1. Peel the celeriac and chop into ½–¾ in (1–2 cm) cubes. Mince the garlic and finely chop the shallots.

2. Melt the butter (or heat the oil) in a pot over medium heat. Add the garlic, celeriac and shallot with a good pinch of salt and sweat for about 10 minutes, stirring occasionally.

3. In a jug, dissolve the stock cube in 4¼ cups (1 liter) of boiling water. Drain and rinse the cannellini beans. Add the stock and beans to the pot. Tie the thyme sprigs together with a piece of food-safe string and add to the pot. Bring to a boil, then reduce the heat to low and gently simmer for 20–25 minutes or until the celeriac has softened.

4. While the soup is cooking, make the gremolata. Lightly toast the almonds in a dry pan over medium heat for 4–5 minutes until golden. Lightly crush some of the toasted almonds into a bowl with your fingers, leaving about half of them whole. Finely chop the preserved lemon and parsley, then add to the bowl, along with a few twists of pepper and the olive oil. Taste and adjust. You won't need salt if you've used preserved lemon, but if you've used fresh lemon, make sure to season well with salt.

5. When the soup has finished cooking, remove the thyme from the pot and discard. Pour the soup into a blender and add the milk, almond butter and vegan cream cheese, if using. Blend until smooth, then taste and adjust the seasonings. Add more plant-based milk if you prefer a thinner consistency. Pour it back into the pot to heat through, if necessary.

6. To serve, ladle the soup into bowls and top generously with the gremolata, plenty of pepper and chile flakes, if you like.

● GLUTEN-FREE

Ginger & Miso Noodle Soup

I really love noodle soups because they're infinitely customizable. You can throw in whatever you have on hand and, with a few pantry essentials, you have a soup. I love adding kimchi to my broth to add a zing of flavor and to look after my gut health.

SERVES 2
20 minutes

INGREDIENTS

2 TBSP (25 G)	Fresh root ginger	
2	Garlic cloves	
1 TBSP	Sesame oil	
1	Vegetable stock cube	
1 TSP	Light or dark soy sauce	
1 OZ (35 G)	Dried shiitake mushrooms (whole or sliced)	
2 OZ (60 G)	Dark leafy greens, such as bok choi, kale or spinach	
1 LB (500 G)	Vegan noodles (I used udon)	
2 TBSP	White miso paste	
10½ OZ (300 G)	Silken tofu	
4 TBSP	Vegan kimchi (optional)	
2 TBSP	Sesame seeds (optional)	
1 OZ (25 G)	Package of nori sheets	

1. Peel and grate the ginger and garlic.

2. Heat the oil in a medium-sized pot over low heat. Add the ginger and garlic and fry gently for 2–3 minutes, stirring often, until fragrant but not browned.

3. Add 4¼ cups (1 liter) of water, along with the stock cube, soy sauce and the dried shiitake. Increase the heat and bring to a boil, then reduce the heat to low and simmer gently for 5 minutes. Now stir in your greens. Check how long your noodles take to cook add them to the broth for that amount of time.

4. Remove a ladleful of broth and pour it into a small bowl. Add the miso to the bowl and whisk well until fully incorporated. Pour this back into the pot and stir.

5. Cut the silken tofu into small cubes and add these to the broth.

6. To serve, ladle the broth and noodles into bowls and top with the kimchi and sesame seeds, if using. Crumble a couple of nori sheets over each bowl and enjoy.

● NUT-FREE

Speedy Chickpea & Harissa Soup

I wanted to make the speediest, easiest soup possible, for those days when you just want something filling and healthy but also delicious. This checks all those boxes and happens to be made with pantry staples, so keep them all on hand and you can whip up this soup in no time.

SERVES 4
15 minutes

INGREDIENTS

14 OZ (400 G)	Can of whole or chopped tomatoes
2–4 TSP	Harissa paste (depending on how spicy you like it), plus extra to serve
2	Roasted red peppers from a jar
1 TSP	Tomato paste
2 TBSP	Tahini, plus extra to serve
2 × 14 OZ (400 G)	Cans of chickpeas
1¾ OZ (50 G)	Spinach (optional)
2 TBSP	Toasted sesame seeds
–	Handful of flat-leaf parsley
–	Salt and freshly ground black pepper

1. Tip the tomatoes, harissa, red peppers, tomato paste and tahini into a blender. Add one of the cans of chickpeas and blend until smooth, then transfer to a pot over medium-high heat. Add the remaining chickpeas. Fill the tomato can with water and pour it into the pan. Stir to combine, then cook on medium heat for 10 minutes.

2. Use a fork or potato masher to mash the chickpeas a little. They should have a chunky texture and some can still be whole. Add the spinach now, if using. Heat gently for a few minutes more until just bubbling. Season well with salt and pepper.

3. To serve, drizzle a little tahini and harissa over the top, then finish a sprinkling of sesame seeds and parsley.

● GLUTEN-FREE ● NUT-FREE

This chapter is all about simplicity, with minimal effort and dish-washing. Most of the recipes in this chapter are full, balanced meals on their own, while a few are quick and easy side dishes. To make sure you aren't missing out on flavor, lots of recipes involve roasting in layers or stages, getting that char and depth that takes each ingredient to the next level.

One-Pot Miso Mushroom Pasta Bake

Peanut butter might seem an odd addition to a one-pot pasta dish, but it adds a decadent creaminess and a mild nutty flavor. It magically turns into a creamy sauce that cooks the pasta perfectly, transforming a few simple ingredients into a rich, saucy, umami flavor-bomb.

SERVES 4
45 minutes

INGREDIENTS

10½ OZ (300 G)	Mushrooms (button, shiitake, crimini, oyster or a mix)
3	Garlic cloves
1	Red onion
1	Vegetable stock cube
2 TBSP	White miso paste
⅓ CUP (85 G)	Smooth peanut butter
½ OZ (15 G)	Dried mushrooms (optional)
8 OZ (225 G)	Paccheri pasta or another short pasta shape, like farfalle/fusilli
3½ OZ (100 G)	Spinach
—	Zest and juice of 1 lemon
—	Salt, freshly ground black pepper and olive oil

1. Preheat the oven to 400°F (200°C).

2. Chop the mushrooms into bite-sized pieces and add to a large casserole dish or roasting pan.

3. Mince the garlic and slice the onion and add these to the mushrooms. Drizzle over some olive oil and season with salt and pepper. Roast for 15 minutes, tossing once in that time.

4. Meanwhile, pour 3⅓ cups (800 ml) of boiling water into a heatproof jug. Add the stock cube, miso, peanut butter and dried mushrooms, if using. Season with plenty of pepper and whisk to combine.

5. When the mushrooms are ready, remove them from the oven and increase the oven temperature to 425°F (220°C).

6. Pour the broth into the dish or pan with the mushrooms. Add the pasta and stir to combine, trying to push the pasta into the water as much as possible. Cover with a lid or wrap the top very tightly with foil. Return to the oven and bake for 15 minutes, then remove the lid, add the spinach and stir well, before covering once more and baking for another 10 minutes. Check that the pasta is cooked to your liking and put it back in the oven for 3–5 minutes more if needed.

7. When it's ready, stir through a good squeeze of lemon juice and finish with some lemon zest, then serve.

Eggplant & Freekeh Pie

Freekeh is a young, cracked durum wheat grain with a uniquely smoky, nutty taste. It's popular in Middle Eastern and North African cuisines and is another nutrient-dense, vitamin-packed grain that's a great addition to a well-stocked pantry. If you can't find it, bulgur, farro or barley will all work well in this hearty, healthy pie.

SERVES 6–8
1 hour

INGREDIENTS

1 CUP (100 G)	Cashews
2	Eggplants
1–2 TBSP	Harissa paste (depending on how spicy you like it)
2	Onions
3	Garlic cloves
1¼ CUPS (200 G)	Freekeh
2 TBSP	Tomato paste
½	Vegetable stock cube
14 OZ (400 G)	Can of chopped tomatoes
⅓ CUP (20 G)	Flat-leaf parsley
1 TBSP	Sherry vinegar
3	Filo pastry sheets
—	Olive oil

1. Preheat the oven to 425°F (220°C).

2. Place the cashews on a baking sheet and toast in the oven for 5–7 minutes until golden, shaking halfway.

3. Chop the eggplants into small cubes and place in a roasting pan. Add 4 tablespoons of olive oil and the harissa and mix well to combine. Roast for 25–30 minutes, until golden and charred on the edges.

4. Finely chop the onions and mince the garlic. Rinse the freekeh. Heat a drizzle of olive oil in a large pot over medium heat. Add the onions and sauté for about 8 minutes until translucent. Add the freekeh, garlic and tomato paste, and cook for 2–3 minutes until fragrant. Now add the stock cube and canned tomatoes. Fill the tomato tin with water and add that, too. Bring to a boil, then reduce the heat to low and simmer for 10 minutes.

5. Finely chop the parsley.

6. Add the eggplants to the freekeh, along with the sherry vinegar and most of the toasted cashews and chopped parsley (saving some for garnish). Season well, then pour the mixture into a medium-sized baking dish.

7. Scrunch the filo sheets over the top and brush each layer with olive oil. Bake for 25 minutes on the bottom rack of the oven.

8. Scatter the remaining cashews and parsley on top before serving.

Spiced Baked Dal with Butternut Squash

For this chapter, I wanted to create easy, complete, balanced meals with minimal fuss and dish-washing, without compromising on flavor. This baked dal checks all the boxes. Serve with rice or fluffy flatbreads, or both.

SERVES 4

1 hour

INGREDIENTS

1 TBSP	Cumin seeds (or ¾ tbsp ground cumin)
1 TBSP	Coriander seeds (or ¾ tbsp ground coriander)
4	Small banana shallots
1	Head of garlic
2	Red chiles
3 TBSP (40 G)	Fresh root ginger
½ TSP	Ground turmeric
1–3 TSP	Chile powder
3 TSP	Curry powder
6 TBSP	Olive oil
1	Small butternut squash (1 lb 10 oz/750 g)
1	Orange
1 CUP (200 G)	Red split lentils
1	Vegetable stock cube (gluten-free if needed)
14 OZ (400 ML)	Can of full-fat coconut milk
14 OZ (400 G)	Can of chopped tomatoes
1 TBSP	Maple syrup
—	Salt and freshly ground black pepper
—	Small bunch of cilantro, to garnish
3–4 TBSP	Soy or coconut yogurt (optional), to garnish

1. Preheat the oven to 425°F (220°C).

2. Grind the cumin and coriander seeds using a mortar and pestle. Peel the shallots and thickly slice lengthways. Halve the head of garlic widthways. Halve one of the chiles lengthways, remove the seeds and cut into thin slices. Peel and finely chop the ginger. Add it all to a large baking dish, with the turmeric, 1–2 teaspoons of the chile powder, 2 teaspoons of the curry powder and 3 tablespoons of the olive oil. Toss and roast for 10 minutes.

3. Meanwhile, peel the squash and slice into ½ in (1.5 cm) thick half-moons. Place in a large bowl. Halve the orange. Set one half aside and cut the other half into quarters. Add these to the bowl. Sprinkle over the remaining 1 teaspoon of curry powder and 1 teaspoon of chile powder, and drizzle over 2 tablespoons of the olive oil. Season with plenty of salt and pepper.

4. Meanwhile, rinse the lentils well. Finely chop the cilantro and the remaining chile and set aside.

5. When the shallots are ready, remove the garlic from the dish and set aside. Add the lentils to the dish, along with 1½ cups (350 ml) of boiling water, the stock cube, the coconut milk (save a little) and the chopped tomatoes. Stir well. Add plenty of salt and pepper and stir again.

6. Arrange the butternut squash and orange pieces over the lentils and nestle the garlic into the dish. Cover tightly with foil and bake for 25 minutes. Remove the foil, drizzle over the maple syrup and a final tablespoon of olive oil, and bake for 15 minutes, uncovered.

7. Remove the dish from the oven. Squeeze the garlic out of its skin into the lentils, and squeeze over the juice from the remaining orange half. Stir well to combine. Spoon the reserved coconut milk and the yogurt (if using) on top. Sprinkle on the cilantro and fresh chile to serve.

● GLUTEN-FREE   ● NUT-FREE

Cauliflower Pie with Crispy Quinoa Crust

Crispy quinoa is arguably better than non-crispy quinoa, and this pie crust is made of just that. The silken tofu filling is a creamy vessel that carries the roasted cauliflower and caramelized onions. It makes a perfect packed lunch or healthy, high-protein dinner.

SERVES 6-8
1 hour 30 minutes

FOR THE CRUST

1 CUP (180 G)	Quinoa
1	Vegetable stock cube (gluten-free if needed)
2 TBSP	Ground flaxseed

FOR THE FILLING

2	Red onions
1	Small cauliflower (1 lb 2 oz/550 g)
10½ OZ (300 G)	Silken tofu
2 TBSP	Chickpea flour
2 TBSP	Nutritional yeast
2 TSP	Dijon mustard
½ TSP	Garlic powder
—	Salt, freshly ground black pepper and olive oil

TIPS
YOU'LL NEED A 10 IN (25 CM) TART PAN, IDEALLY ONE WITH A LOOSE BASE. THIS WILL KEEP IN THE FRIDGE FOR 3-4 DAYS.

1. Preheat the oven to 400°F (200°C). Line the base of your tart pan with parchment paper and lightly grease the sides.

2. Rinse the quinoa and add to a pot with plenty of cold water and the stock cube. Bring to a boil, then reduce the heat to low and leave to simmer, covered, for 10 minutes. Drain, then tip the quinoa onto a tray or large plate and spread it out to cool. You can do this the day before and keep it in the fridge.

3. In a small bowl, mix the ground flax with 2 tablespoons of cold water and set aside.

4. To begin preparing the filling, finely slice the onions. Heat 2 tablespoons of olive oil in a large frying pan over medium heat. Add the onions and season with salt and pepper. Fry for about 15 minutes on medium heat until softened but not crispy.

5. Cut the cauliflower into bite-sized pieces and tip into a roasting pan. Drizzle with olive oil and season with salt and pepper. Roast for 25 minutes, tossing halfway.

6. Drain the tofu and tip it into a blender with the chickpea flour, nutritional yeast, mustard and garlic powder. Add 1 tablespoon of oil and plenty of salt and pepper, and process until smooth.

7. To make the crust, combine the quinoa and flaxseed mixture in a large bowl and season well with salt and pepper. Use your hands to squeeze it together. Knead it so that it breaks down slightly and becomes congealed. It should hold together in big pieces if you squeeze it in your hand. Push the quinoa mixture into the bottom and sides of the prepared pan, and bake for 25 minutes.

8. Remove from the oven and pour the tofu mixture into the crust. Mix the caramelized onions and cauliflower and scatter evenly over the tofu. Return to the oven and bake for 25 minutes on the bottom rack. Allow to cool for 10 minutes before serving.

● GLUTEN-FREE   ● NUT-FREE

Garlic Baked Orzo with Crispy Kale

This is my favorite easy side dish, perfect to serve with roasted veggies and a big hearty salad. The crispy kale on the top brings that extra layer of crunch as well as a great way to get some greens in. I like to make this super garlicky but feel free to use the lesser amount and tone it down.

SERVES 4
30 minutes

INGREDIENTS

2–6	Garlic cloves
2	Vegetable stock cubes
1⅓ CUPS (300 G)	Orzo
3½ OZ (100 G)	Kale
—	Salt, freshly ground black pepper and olive oil

1. Preheat the oven to 400°F (200°C).

2. Pour 3 cups (750 ml) of boiling water into a measuring jug. Mince the garlic cloves and add these to the water, along with the stock cubes, and stir to dissolve.

3. Tip the orzo into a medium-sized baking dish and pour over the stock. Stir, then cover tightly with foil and bake for 15 minutes.

4. Meanwhile, remove any tough stems from the kale, tear into bite-sized pieces and place in a bowl. Drizzle over some olive oil and season well with salt and pepper. Lightly massage the oil and salt and pepper into the kale so it breaks down a little.

5. After the 15 minutes of cooking, remove the orzo from the oven and remove the foil. Drizzle ½ tablespoon of olive oil over the orzo and stir well. Scatter the kale over the top and return to the oven to bake, uncovered, for 10 more minutes.

6. This is great served hot or at room temperature. Any leftovers can be stored in the fridge for up to 3 days, but the crispy kale topping is best enjoyed fresh.

Leek & Cannellini Bean Gratin with Oat & Hazelnut Crumbs

This is a great example of how beans can be used to add creaminess. When blended with the right ingredients (miso and nutritional yeast for flavor, and nuts or seeds for healthy fats), the result is a surprisingly decadent, creamy filling that works perfectly with the caramelized leeks and hazelnut crumbs.

SERVES 4-6
50 minutes

INGREDIENTS

4	Leeks (about 1 lb 5 oz/600 g)
14 OZ (400 G)	Can of cannellini beans
—	Zest of 1 lemon
—	Salt, freshly ground black pepper and olive oil

FOR THE CREAM

14 OZ (400 G)	Can of cannellini beans
2-3	Garlic cloves
3 TBSP	Nutritional yeast
½ CUP (50 G)	Cashews (or sunflower seeds or tahini)
1 TBSP	White miso paste
⅔ CUP (150 ML)	Unsweetened oat milk
4 TSP	Olive oil

FOR THE OAT HAZELNUT CRUMBS

½ CUP (80 G)	Hazelnuts
1-2	Rosemary sprigs (or use your favorite dried mixed herbs)
5 TBSP (70 G)	Vegan butter, chilled
1 CUP (120 G)	Oats
2-3 TSP	Chile flakes (optional)
½ CUP (50 G)	Grated vegan cheese (optional)

1. Preheat the oven to 425°F (220°C).

2. Trim the leeks, then halve lengthways and cut into roughly ¾ in (2 cm) pieces. Place in a baking dish and drizzle with olive oil. Season with salt and pepper. Cover tightly with foil and roast for 20 minutes, then remove the foil and roast for another 10 minutes.

3. Meanwhile, make the cream. Empty the cannellini beans, along with their liquid, into a blender. Add the remaining cream ingredients and season with plenty of salt and pepper. Blend until smooth.

4. To make the oat hazelnut crumbs, roughly chop the hazelnuts and finely chop the rosemary. Add to a bowl. Chop the cold butter into small pieces and add to the bowl, along with the oats and chile flakes, if using. Season with a little salt and pepper. Add the vegan cheese, if using. Use your fingertips to mix everything together into crumbs.

5. When the leeks have finished roasting, drain the second can of beans and add them to the baking dish with the leeks. Season with salt and pepper and give everything a toss. Now pour the cream into the baking dish and stir well to evenly combine. Scatter over the oat crumbs and top with a few twists of pepper, then bake on the middle rack for 15 minutes.

6. Finish with some lemon zest and allow to cool down slightly before serving.

Mushroom & Root Vegetable Centerpiece

This is a real showpiece that takes a little effort but is so worth it. It looks beautiful but is also jam-packed with flavors, textures, colors and nutrients. I love making this for a festive table, but it's also a great Sunday lunch treat.

SERVES 8-10
2 hours

INGREDIENTS

1¼ CUPS (250 G)	Cooked lentils, or ⅔ cup (125 g) uncooked lentils (ideally a small variety such as puy, beluga or small green lentils)
2 TBSP	Vegan butter, plus extra for greasing
1 HEAPED TBSP	Ground flaxseed
2 LB 4 OZ (1 KG)	Crimini or button mushrooms
3-4	Thyme sprigs
1 CUP (115 G)	Walnuts
6	Garlic cloves
4	Shallots
2 TBSP	Balsamic vinegar
1 TBSP	Light soy sauce (or tamari if gluten-free)
7 OZ (200 G)	Vegan cream cheese (gluten-free if needed)
1 SMALL	Celeriac (celery root)
1	Large beet
1 TSP	Miso paste
2 TBSP	Vegan mayonnaise
1 TSP	Wholegrain mustard
—	Juice of 1 lemon
—	Pomegranate seeds (optional, for garnish)
—	Handful of parsley or dill
—	Salt, freshly ground black pepper and olive oil

1. Cook the lentils if you are not using pre-cooked lentils.

2. Preheat the oven to 400°F (200°C). Grease the sides of an 8-9 in (20-23 cm) cake pan with some vegan butter and line the bottom with parchment paper.

3. In a small bowl, mix the ground flaxseed with 3 tablespoons of water. Set aside.

4. Roughly chop the mushrooms and pick the leaves off the thyme sprigs.

5. Toast the walnuts in a dry frying pan over medium-low heat for about 6 minutes, then finely chop or pulse in a food processor to a coarse texture. Set aside.

6. Mince the garlic and finely dice the shallots. Melt the butter in a saucepan over medium heat. Add the shallots and cook for 7-8 minutes until translucent, then add the garlic and sauté for 2 minutes more.

7. Add the mushrooms and thyme and increase the heat to medium-high. Sweat them down for about 15 minutes until all the moisture has evaporated. You might need to split the mixture between two pans for this, as you don't want to overcrowd the mushrooms in one pan. They need plenty of space to caramelize.

8. Add the balsamic vinegar and soy sauce, and stir for a few minutes until they evaporate. Season well.

9. Add the flaxseed mixture, along with the walnuts, lentils and 2 tablespoons of the cream cheese. Check the seasoning.

CONTINUED OVERLEAF

● GLUTEN-FREE

RECIPE CONTINUED

10   Spoon the mushroom mixture into the prepared pan and use the back of a spoon to even out the surface. Pop the cake pan onto a baking sheet, as it may leak. Bake for 30 minutes until golden brown on top.

11   While the mushroom bake is in the oven, peel and thinly slice the celeriac and beet. Use a mandoline if you have one, or a very sharp knife. Try to slice them about ⅛ in (3 mm) thick.

12   Put the celeriac and beet slices into two separate roasting pans. Season well and drizzle with olive oil, tossing to make sure that each slice is evenly coated. Cover tightly with foil and roast for 20 minutes until soft and supple enough to crumple.

13   In a small bowl, mix together the miso, mayonnaise and mustard and a squeeze of lemon juice, until smooth.

14   In a separate bowl, mix the rest of the cream cheese with 4 teaspoons of the miso mayo mustard and a squeeze of lemon juice. Taste and add a little more mustard or lemon if you like.

15   When the mushroom bake is ready, set aside to cool for 15 minutes before removing from the cake pan and leave to cool completely. Once the bake has cooled, spread the cream cheese mixture over the top with the back of a spoon, taking care not to scrape off the top of the bake.

16   Next, scrunch the pieces of celeriac and beet and place them one by one onto the cream cheese. Arrange them close to one another so that they hold their shape. Continue until you have covered the whole top of the bake.

17   Finally, drizzle the miso mayo mustard all over the top, then finish with a sprinkle of pomegranate seeds, if you like, and parsley or dill, and serve.

Spanakopita

Spinach pie is a Greek and Cypriot classic, found in every bakery on every corner. It comes in many shapes and sizes, and this is my easy version, simply layered into a baking dish.

SERVES 4–6
55 minutes

INGREDIENTS

1	Onion
1	Leek (or use 4 scallions)
2	Garlic cloves
¼ CUP (15 G)	Flat-leaf parsley
1 TBSP (5 G)	Mint leaves
¼ CUP (5 G)	Dill
2 LB 4 OZ (1 KG)	Fresh or frozen spinach, thawed if using frozen (see Tip)
—	Juice of ½ lemon
9½ OZ (270 G)	Filo pastry
—	Sesame seeds, nigella seeds or onion seeds, for the topping (optional)
—	Salt, freshly ground black pepper and olive oil

FOR THE TOFU

10½ OZ (300 G)	Firm tofu
½ TSP	Garlic powder
3 TBSP	Nutritional yeast
—	Juice of 1 lemon
2 TSP	Salt

TIP

IF YOU'RE USING FROZEN SPINACH, MAKE SURE IT'S NOT CHOPPED. THAW THE SPINACH BEFORE USE. YOU CAN EITHER LET IT THAW ON THE COUNTER, IN THE MICROWAVE OR IN A LARGE PAN ON THE STOVE. WRING OUT AS MUCH LIQUID FROM THE SPINACH AS POSSIBLE. I USUALLY SQUEEZE HANDFULS OVER THE SINK.

1 Preheat the oven to 400°F (200°C).

2 Pat the tofu dry with a paper towel and crumble it into a bowl, making sure that the pieces are not too small, as they will break up further later on. Stir through the garlic powder, nutritional yeast, lemon juice and salt.

3 Dice the onion and finely slice the leek. Grate or mince the garlic. Remove any tough stems from the herbs, then crush them by rolling them in your hands to release their flavor. Finely chop, then set aside.

4 Heat a good drizzle of olive oil in a frying pan over medium heat. Add the leek, onion and garlic, and season with salt and pepper. Fry for 10–12 minutes until translucent but not brown.

5 Add the spinach and cook for another 3–4 minutes to combine the flavors. If you're using fresh spinach, you will need to add it a handful at a time, letting it wilt down between additions. It's important that the mixture is as dry as possible to avoid a soggy filo, so keep cooking gently if a little water remains.

6 Take the pan off the heat and add the fresh herbs and a squeeze of lemon juice, along with another drizzle of olive oil.

7 Carefully stir the tofu into the spinach mixture. Season with salt and pepper, adding more than you usually would as both the spinach and tofu need it.

CONTINUED OVERLEAF

NUT-FREE

RECIPE CONTINUED

8. Lay out the pastry sheets and place a clean tea towel on top to prevent them from drying out. Brush a medium-large baking dish with some olive oil, then line the base of the dish with a layer of pastry sheets, letting the excess hang over the short sides. Drizzle or brush with some more olive oil and add another layer of pastry, but this time hanging the excess over one long edge. Brush with more olive oil and add another layer of pastry, this time hanging the excess over the opposite side. This means you should have some excess pastry hanging over each of the 4 sides of the baking dish.

9. Top the pastry with the spinach mixture and flatten down. Add 4 more pastry layers over the spinach, brushing each sheet with olive oil and pushing the excess pastry into the sides. Fold the overhanging pastry sheets from the bottom over the top pastry sheets and push into the edges. Trim any areas where the pastry seems too thick.

10. Brush all over with a little more oil and sprinkle with the seeds, if using, and a little salt.

11. Bake on the bottom rack of the oven for 20–30 minutes, or until golden brown all over. Leave it to set for 10 minutes before serving. This will keep in the fridge for up to 3 days and is delicious served cold or warmed up in the oven.

Slow-Roasted Veggie Gnocchi

This simple one-pan dish is full of textures, flavor and is pure comfort food. The slow-roasted, almost confit vegetables melt into each other to become a delicious sauce. I've used gnocchi here, but another pasta or even butter beans would work just as well. The herby drizzle breaks up the mellow flavors, but if you decide to skip it, a little lemon zest and juice would do the trick.

SERVES 4
1 hour

INGREDIENTS

2	Eggplants
2	Zucchinis
2–3	Large tomatoes (or 2 big handfuls of cherry tomatoes)
4	Garlic cloves
1 LB (500 G)	Gnocchi
—	Salt, freshly ground black pepper and olive oil

FOR THE HERB DRIZZLE

½ CUP (25 G)	Fresh herbs (such as parsley, basil, dill, chives or a mix), plus extra for garnish
—	Zest and juice of ½ lemon
1–2 TSP	Chile flakes (optional)

1. Preheat the oven to 410°F (210°C).

2. Pierce the eggplants and zucchinis all over with a fork. Place in a baking dish and drizzle with 4–5 tablespoons of olive oil. Season with salt and pepper and roast for 25 minutes.

3. Meanwhile, make the herb drizzle. Finely chop the herbs or blend in a small food processor. Add the lemon zest and juice, and chile flakes, if using. Season with salt and pepper and add enough olive oil for a drizzle-able consistency, about 3 tablespoons. Set aside.

4. Remove the baking dish from the oven and add the tomatoes and garlic cloves. Pour in enough olive oil to just cover the garlic cloves. Sprinkle some more salt and pepper over the new vegetables, and roast for another 25 minutes until everything is very soft and maybe starting to char. Use a fork to check the eggplants, zucchinis and tomatoes are done by pushing them down softly; they should squash down with almost no force.

5. Remove from the oven. Slice open the zucchinis and eggplants and scoop out the flesh into the dish. Use two forks to pull apart the remaining skin, tearing it into small pieces. Do the same with the tomato. Squash the garlic cloves and mix through.

6. Tip in the gnocchi and stir it into the vegetables. The dish should now look like a juicy, chunky vegetable sauce, but if it's looking a little dry, add a splash of water or olive oil. Put it back into the oven and bake for 5 minutes. Taste and season again if needed. It might seem like a lot of salt and pepper, but the vegetables release a lot of water, so they really need the extra seasoning.

7. To serve, ladle the gnocchi and veggies into bowls and finish with the herb drizzle and some fresh herbs, if you like.

One-Pot Mushroom Lasagne

For this one-pot classic, I've removed all the laborious layering but kept all the flavor. Broken lasagne sheets cook in the rich, tomatoey sauce for an easy, updated version of this beloved dish.

SERVES 6
1 hour 15 minutes

INGREDIENTS

2	Onions
1 LB 9 OZ (700 G)	Crimini or portobellini mushrooms
8–10	Garlic cloves
3 OZ (80 G)	Sun-dried tomatoes, plus 2 tbsp oil from the jar
¾ CUP (150 G)	Puy lentils
2	Vegetable stock cubes
2 TBSP	Tomato paste
2–4 TBSP	Harissa paste
2 × 14 OZ (400 G)	Cans of plum tomatoes
12	Dried lasagne sheets
5½ OZ (150 G)	Vegan cheese (nut-free if needed)
—	Salt and freshly ground black pepper

TIP
YOU'LL NEED A LARGE CASSEROLE DISH WITH A LID FOR THIS RECIPE. I USED A 12½ IN (32 CM) SHALLOW CAST-IRON DISH, BUT IF YOU PREFER, YOU CAN USE A PAN FOR THE FRYING AND THEN TRANSFER IT TO A BAKING DISH, WRAPPED TIGHTLY IN FOIL, FOR THE OVEN PART.

1. Preheat the oven to 410°F (210°C).

2. Finely chop the onions and mushrooms, or use a food processor to pulse in batches. Take care not to over-process; you don't want them to turn into pulp. Finely chop or grate the garlic. Roughly chop the sun-dried tomatoes. Rinse the lentils.

3. Heat the oil from the sun-dried tomatoes in a shallow Dutch oven (or pan) over medium heat. Add the onions and garlic and sauté for about 5 minutes until softened and translucent. Now add the mushrooms and sun-dried tomatoes. Season well with salt and pepper, and sauté for 8–10 minutes until the mushrooms are starting to brown and caramelize and the liquid has evaporated.

4. Meanwhile, pour 4¼ cups (1 liter) of boiling water into a jug. Add the stock cubes and stir to dissolve.

5. Return to the mushrooms. Add the tomato paste, harissa and plum tomatoes, crushing them into the pan with the back of a fork. Add the lentils, followed by three-quarters of the stock. Season well with salt and pepper, and stir. Increase the heat to medium-high and cook for 10 minutes, partly covered with the lid so that steam can still escape. Stir occasionally.

6. Add the rest of the stock and stir well. Break up the lasagne sheets into large pieces and add to the pan, pushing them down so they're submerged. Cover with the lid (or transfer to a baking dish) and put in the oven for 30 minutes.

7. After 30 minutes, remove the pan from the oven and give everything a good stir. Check that the pasta and lentils have cooked through; they should have a firm bite but should not taste powdery or tough. If they need more time, add a splash of water and return to the oven for another 5–10 minutes.

8. When the pasta and lentils are cooked to your liking, sprinkle the cheese over the top and cover once more. Return to the oven for a final 10 minutes or until the cheese has melted, then remove the lid and place under the broiler for a few minutes to crisp up the top, keeping a close eye on it so it doesn't burn. Let the lasagne rest for 10 minutes before serving.

● NUT-FREE

Baked Mushroom Tacos

This tasty taco bake is a great weeknight dinner option. Perfectly seasoned mushrooms that are both crispy and juicy; zingy pickled zucchini; and limey pea purée for some protein-packed creaminess.

SERVES 2, OR 4 WITH SIDES
45 minutes

INGREDIENTS

2-3	Garlic cloves
1	Onion
1 LB 7 OZ (650 G)	Mixed mushrooms (oyster, king oyster, portobello and button)
2	Zucchinis
1	Small red chile
–	Juice of 2 limes
4-6	Tortilla wraps
–	Salt and freshly ground black pepper
–	Plain vegan yogurt (nut-free if needed)
–	hot sauce, to serve

FOR THE SPICE MIX

1 TSP	Ground cumin
¼ TSP	Ground allspice
1 TSP	Ground coriander
½ TBSP	Dried oregano
½ TSP	Smoked paprika
1 TSP	Tomato paste
2 TBSP	Light soy sauce
1 TBSP	Maple syrup
¼–½ TSP	Chile powder
4 TBSP	Olive oil
½ TSP	Flaky sea salt

FOR THE LIMEY PEAS

1½ CUPS (200 G)	Frozen peas
¼ CUP (5 G)	Cilantro leaves
1 OZ (25 G)	Tahini
–	Zest and juice of 3 limes
2 TSP	Olive oil
–	Chile powder (optional)

1. Preheat the oven to 425°F (220°C) and line a large baking sheet with parchment paper.

2. Mix all the spice mix ingredients together in a small bowl.

3. Grate the garlic and finely slice the onion. Pull apart the oyster mushrooms and shred the king oyster mushrooms with a fork, and slice the portobello and button mushrooms. Combine the mushrooms, garlic and onion on the prepared pan. Add the spice mix and some black pepper and mix well to combine.

4. Bake for 30 minutes, tossing every 10 minutes to make sure the mushrooms cook evenly. They should be slightly crispy at the edges. Add a little olive oil if they are looking a bit dry (mushrooms that are slightly older will contain less moisture).

5. Meanwhile, pickle the zucchinis. Use a speed peeler to peel the zucchinis into ribbons and place in a bowl. Finely slice the chile (deseed it if you prefer less heat) and add to the zucchinis, along with the lime juice and a good pinch of salt. Toss well and set aside to soften.

6. To make the limey peas, defrost the peas in a bowl of hot water for a few minutes, then drain. Roughly chop the cilantro. Add the peas to a small food processor, along with the tahini, cilantro leaves, lime zest and juice, and olive oil. Season well with salt and pepper and blend until almost smooth. Add to a bowl and top with a little chile powder, if you like.

7. Heat the tortillas over an open flame or in a hot, dry frying pan.

8. To serve, layer up a tortilla with mushrooms, pea purée and pickled zucchinis, then top with a little cilantro, along with some yogurt and hot sauce, if you like. Enjoy.

● NUT-FREE

Oven-Roasted Mushroom Risotto

This is my foolproof method for the creamiest risotto, with just a few simple ingredients. The trick is to add plenty of oat milk at the end, along with some miso and nutritional yeast for flavor. These combine with the starch from the rice to make a velvety, creamy risotto. You'll need a large, deep, ovenproof pan with a lid, or use a frying pan and transfer to a baking dish covered with foil.

SERVES 6
45 minutes

INGREDIENTS

2	Shallots
4	Garlic cloves
14 OZ (400 G)	Oyster mushrooms (or you can use crimini or portobello)
4–5	Thyme sprigs
1–2 TBSP	Vegan butter (nut-free if needed)
3	Vegetable stock cubes (gluten-free if needed)
2¾ CUPS (600 G)	Arborio rice
2 CUPS (500 ML)	Unsweetened oat milk (or soy milk if gluten-free)
1–2 TBSP	White miso paste
3 TBSP	Nutritional yeast
—	Handful of flat-leaf parsley leaves, to garnish
—	Salt, freshly ground black pepper and olive oil

TIP
I'VE TOPPED THIS WITH MUSHROOMS, BUT YOU CAN USE ANY VEGETABLE YOU LIKE: BUTTERNUT SQUASH, ASPARAGUS, PEAS, ZUCCHINIS AND ROASTED CHERRY TOMATOES ALL WORK GREAT.

1. Preheat the oven to 425°F (220°C).

2. Finely chop the shallots and garlic. Shred the mushrooms by tearing into smaller pieces (if using crimini or portobello, slice them). Add to a baking sheet with a couple of the thyme sprigs. Drizzle with olive oil and season well. Set aside.

3. Heat 1 heaped tablespoon of the butter in an ovenproof frying pan over medium heat. Add the shallot and fry for 4 minutes until translucent, then add the garlic and 2 tablespoons of olive oil and sauté for 3–4 minutes until softened and fragrant. Take care the onion and garlic don't catch and start to brown.

4. Pour 6⅓ cups (1.5 liters) of boiling water into a jug. Add the stock cubes and stir to dissolve.

5. Add the rice to the pan and stir to make sure it's all covered and glossy. Slowly add the stock, stirring constantly. Add a few thyme sprigs on top. Bring to a boil, then cover the pan with the lid and bake for 18 minutes. Stir once at the 10-minute mark.

6. Roast the mushrooms at the same time, for 15–18 minutes or until golden and crispy, tossing halfway through to help them cook evenly (at the same time you stir the risotto).

7. Once the 18 minutes are up, the rice should be cooked through but still have a firm bite. Remove the thyme sprigs.

8. Warm the oat milk with a splash of boiling water to bring it to room temperature, if it isn't already. Whisk in the miso until combined and smooth. Stir the milk through the risotto slowly until you reach the consistency and creaminess you like—you may not use it all. Add the nutritional yeast and season to taste with salt and pepper. If you like, add another tablespoon of butter to make it richer. Top the risotto with the roasted mushrooms and finish with a sprinkle of parsley.

● GLUTEN-FREE ● NUT-FREE

Saucy Eggplant, Chickpea & Tomato Bake

This is a dish that really shows the overlap between Mediterranean and Middle Eastern cuisines and flavors. It's inspired by the Arabic musaqa'a, with similar flavors and ingredients to the Greek and Cypriot moussaka—and it's not too far off from Sicilian caponata. It can be eaten warm or cold, and is perfect served with garlic rice and a fresh, crisp salad.

SERVES 4

1 hour 20 minutes

INGREDIENTS

2	Eggplants
2	Zucchinis
1	Onion
8-10	Sun-dried tomatoes
4-6	Garlic cloves
—	Small handful of cilantro leaves, plus extra to garnish
6-10	Pitted black or green olives (optional)
1 TSP	Ground cumin
1 TSP	Chile powder (optional)
2 TBSP	Tomato paste
14 OZ (400 G)	Can of chickpeas, drained
14 OZ (400 G)	Can of chopped tomatoes
½ TBSP	White or brown sugar
2 TSP	Balsamic vinegar
3	Salad tomatoes
—	Salt, freshly ground black pepper and olive oil

TIP

THIS DISH IS EVEN BETTER THE NEXT DAY AS THE FLAVORS ALL COME TOGETHER.

1. Preheat the oven to 400°F (200°C).

2. Slice the eggplants and zucchinis into ¾ in (2 cm) thick rounds and spread out on a baking sheet (use two if they are overlapping too much). Drizzle with oil and season with salt and pepper. Bake for 10 minutes, then flip and bake on the other side for another 10–15 minutes until golden.

3. Meanwhile, make the sauce. Finely chop the onion, then finely chop the sun-dried tomatoes until they almost form a paste. Mince the garlic. Finely chop the cilantro. Roughly chop the olives, if using.

4. Heat a good drizzle of olive oil in a medium-sized pot over medium heat. Add the onion and a pinch of salt and cook for 3–5 minutes until translucent. Add the garlic, cumin, chile powder (if using), sun-dried tomatoes and tomato paste, and cook for 2–3 minutes. Stir in the drained chickpeas, canned tomatoes, sugar and balsamic vinegar. Half-fill the tomato can with water and stir that through, too. Bring to a boil and simmer for 5 minutes, then take off the heat and stir through the cilantro and olives. Taste and adjust seasonings.

5. Slice the tomatoes into ½ in (1.5 cm) thick rounds.

6. Pour the tomato and chickpea sauce into a medium-sized baking dish. Layer the tomato, eggplant and zucchini rounds over the tomato chickpea sauce. There's not really a method to it, and overlapping them is fine.

7. Cover tightly with foil and bake for 20 minutes, then remove the foil and bake for a further 15 minutes. Allow to cool for at least 10 minutes before serving.

● GLUTEN-FREE   ● NUT-FREE

Spiced Roasted Squash with Pomegranate Molasses & Pistachios

When squash is in season, there are so many delicious things to do with it, but serving it with dates, tahini and tangy pomegranate molasses creates a perfect medley of textures and flavors that complement each other so well. Serve this with couscous, bulgur, freekeh, rice or any other whole grain if you like.
If you can't find pomegranate molasses, you can use balsamic glaze instead.

SERVES 2–4
45 minutes

INGREDIENTS

1	Large butternut squash (about 3 lb 5 oz/1.5 kg)
2 × 14 OZ (400 G)	Cans of chickpeas
4 TBSP	Cumin seeds
2 TBSP	Fennel seeds
2 TBSP	Yellow mustard seeds
2 TSP	Coriander seeds
2 TSP	Smoked paprika
2 TBSP	Sesame seeds
1 TBSP	Flaky sea salt, plus extra to serve
4 TBSP	Olive oil, plus extra to serve
¼ CUP (35 G)	Pistachios
—	Handful of flat-leaf parsley
3–4	Medjool dates
4 TBSP	Tahini
2 TBSP	Pomegranate molasses
—	Zest and juice of 1 lemon

1. Preheat the oven to 425°F (220°C).

2. Halve the squash lengthways (no need to peel). Scoop out the seeds and then quarter each half lengthways, so you have eight long pieces. Cut each piece into ¾–1 in (2–3 cm) chunks.

3. Drain and rinse the chickpeas and pat them dry with a clean tea towel, removing any skins that come loose.

4. Add the squash chunks and chickpeas to a large baking pan (use two baking pans if it looks overcrowded—they need space to cook or they will become mushy).

5. Lightly grind all the spices using a mortar and pestle or spice grinder, keeping some intact. You could even leave them all intact if you like; this will give a chunky texture and pops of flavor. Add the spices to a bowl and mix in the sesame seeds, salt and olive oil.

6. Tip the spice mix into the pan(s) with the chickpeas and squash and mix very well, making sure everything is evenly coated. Bake, uncovered, for 20 minutes, then toss and bake for another 15–18 minutes until the chickpeas are slightly crispy and the squash is tender inside and starting to crisp at the edges.

7. Meanwhile, roughly chop the pistachios and parsley. Remove the pits from the dates and tear them into large pieces.

8. Once the squash is cooked, remove the pan(s) from the oven and scatter over the pistachios and dates, then return to the oven for another 2–3 minutes.

9. Drizzle over the tahini and pomegranate molasses, along with some more olive oil, and sprinkle with salt. Add the lemon zest and juice, and scatter over the parsley to finish. Serve.

● GLUTEN-FREE   ● ALLIUM-FREE

Sticky Coconut Rice with Lime & Toasted Coconut

Baking rice like this ensures every grain is perfectly cooked and fluffy, and the addition of coconut milk makes it beautifully tender and fragrant. The toasted coconut flakes are a limey, crispy addition. This is perfect to serve with a stir-fry, saucy dish or roasted veggies.

SERVES 2–4
50 minutes

INGREDIENTS

1¼ CUPS (250 G)	Jasmine rice
14 OZ (400 ML)	Can of coconut milk
½ TSP	Salt, plus extra to taste
1 TSP	White sugar
1½ TBSP (20 G)	Fresh root ginger
½ CUP (50 G)	Unsweetened shredded coconut
—	Zest and juice of 1 lime

1. Preheat the oven to 425°F (220°C).

2. Rinse the rice well and place in a medium-sized baking dish. Pour the coconut milk into the dish. Add the salt and sugar, and stir well to combine. Peel the ginger and pop it into the middle of the rice.

3. Cover tightly with foil and bake for 40 minutes on the middle rack of the oven.

4. Meanwhile, scatter the coconut over a shallow baking sheet and bake for about 4 minutes on the bottom rack, stirring every minute or so. Don't forget about it, as it burns very quickly.

5. Remove the rice from the oven but leave the foil on. Leave it to stand for at least 10 minutes.

6. Remove the foil, then sprinkle the toasted coconut and lime zest and juice over the top. Season with a little salt, and serve.

● GLUTEN-FREE   ● ALLIUM-FREE

Stir-Fry Bake with Tofu & Peanut Drizzle

This is essentially a stir-fry, but baked, meaning you can dump everything on a pan, leave it in the oven and come back to a perfectly cooked meal. You can skip the drizzle if you're really looking for the laziest dinner and make up for it with extra chile oil.

SERVES 2
40 minutes

INGREDIENTS

3	Garlic cloves
—	Thumb-sized piece of fresh root ginger
2 TBSP	Light soy sauce
1 TBSP	Sesame oil, plus extra for drizzling
1 TBSP	Sunflower oil or canola oil
4	Scallions
7 OZ (200 G)	Baby corn
10 OZ (280 G)	Extra-firm tofu
¼ CUP (40 G)	Peanuts
7 OZ (200 G)	Snow peas
10½ OZ (300 G)	Straight-to-wok udon noodles
1	Red chile
2 TBSP	Crispy chile oil or sriracha

FOR THE PEANUT SATAY DRIZZLE

3 TBSP	Peanut butter (crunchy or smooth)
1 TBSP	Light soy sauce
1 TBSP	Sesame oil
—	Juice of 1 lime, plus extra to serve
1 TBSP	Maple syrup

1. Preheat the oven to 425°F (220°C).

2. Mince the garlic and ginger and combine in a small bowl. Add the soy sauce, sesame oil and sunflower oil, and whisk well.

3. Cut off the green parts of the scallions and set them aside for now. Halve the scallion whites lengthways down the middle, then cut each half into 3 pieces.

4. Roughly chop the baby corn into bite-sized rounds. Cut the tofu into bite-sized cubes. Chop the peanuts.

5. Find the biggest baking sheet you have and line it with parchment paper. Use two baking sheets if you don't have a very big one, so you don't overcrowd the vegetables. Spread out the tofu, scallion whites, corn and snow peas over the pan(s). Drizzle over the soy sauce mixture and toss well to make sure everything is evenly coated.

6. Bake for 15 minutes, then toss and bake for another 10 minutes until the tofu is golden and the veggies are cooked and slightly charred. Add the noodles and a drizzle of sesame oil to the tray. Toss to combine, then sprinkle over the chopped peanuts. Return to the oven for another 5 minutes. The noodles should be warmed through and starting to char in spots.

7. Meanwhile, finely slice the reserved scallion greens and the chile.

8. To make the satay drizzle, simply whisk together all the ingredients in a small bowl until smooth.

9. Remove the pan(s) from the oven, and sprinkle over the sliced chile and scallion greens. Spoon over the satay drizzle and crispy chile oil, and squeeze over more lime juice to serve.

Sweet Potato Shepherd's Pie

This is my version of the classic shepherd's pie, with mushrooms, lentils and an optional addition of heat. It's a hearty, homey dish that you can easily customize with whatever you have: think carrots, frozen peas, eggplant or zucchinis.

SERVES 6
1 hour

INGREDIENTS

3 LB 5 OZ (1.5 KG)	Sweet potatoes
¾ CUP (150 G)	Dried lentils (see Tip)
3½ OZ (100 G)	Sun-dried tomatoes, plus 2 tbsp oil from the jar
2	Onions
1 LB 5 OZ (600 G)	Button mushrooms
4–6	Garlic cloves
–	Handful of flat-leaf parsley
⅓ CUP (45 G)	Walnuts
1	Red chile (optional)
14 OZ (400 G)	Can of chopped tomatoes
3 TBSP	Balsamic vinegar
–	Salt, freshly ground black pepper and olive oil

TIPS

USE SMALL FRENCH LENTILS IF YOU CAN, SUCH AS PUY OR BELUGA, AS THEY RETAIN THEIR TEXTURE WHEN COOKED. YOU CAN ALSO USE PRE-COOKED, CANNED OR PACKAGED LENTILS (1½ CUPS/300 G COOKED), BUT DON'T ADD ANY WATER AND SKIP THE COOKING STAGE.

IF YOU LIKE, YOU CAN SWAP THE SWEET POTATOES FOR REGULAR POTATOES OR ANOTHER ROOT VEGETABLE.

KEEP ANY LEFTOVERS IN THE FRIDGE FOR UP TO 3 DAYS OR FREEZE THE PIE IN PORTIONS.

1. Preheat the oven to 400°F (200°C).

2. Scrub the potatoes clean. Peeling is optional; I prefer to leave the skin on as it's full of nutrients and gives a nice texture to the mash. Chop into large pieces (about 1½ in/4 cm chunks). Bring a large pot of salted water to a boil, and boil the potatoes for 15–18 minutes until soft enough to squash easily with a fork. Drain and allow to steam dry in the colander.

3. Cook the lentils in plenty of water for a few minutes less than the package instructions until nicely al dente. The exact time will depend on the type of lentils you use. Drain and set aside.

4. To make the mash, tip the potatoes back into the pot or into another large bowl. Add the 2 tablespoons of oil from the sun-dried tomatoes and mash with a fork or potato masher. I like quite a chunky texture, but you can get them as smooth as you like. Season very well with plenty of salt and pepper.

5. Finely chop the onions and mushrooms, and mince the garlic. Roughly chop the sun-dried tomatoes. Finely chop the parsley and walnuts. Finely chop the chile, if using. Set aside.

6. Heat a good drizzle of olive oil in a large, heavy-based frying pan or pot over medium heat. Add the mushrooms and season with salt and pepper, then fry for 8–10 minutes until golden and softened and starting to brown.

7. Add the onions, garlic and chile, if using, and season with a little more salt and pepper. Cook for another 6–8 minutes, then add the canned tomatoes, balsamic vinegar, sun-dried tomatoes and cooked lentils, followed by the parsley and walnuts. Stir to combine. Taste and season well.

8. Pour the filling into a medium-sized baking dish and spoon over the potatoes. Drizzle with a little olive oil if you like, and bake until the top starts to turn crisp and golden, about 10–15 minutes. Put it under the broiler for 5 minutes to crisp up the top. Serve.

● GLUTEN-FREE

Smoky Pickled Carrot Tart with Everything Bagel Seasoning

This tart has elements of a cream cheese bagel with that famous American "everything bagel" seasoning. The lightly pickled and marinated carrots bring a smoky saltiness, along with a mild flavor of the sea thanks to the nori seaweed and capers. The seasoning is completely optional—if you prefer, you can just use sesame seeds to keep it simple. This is perfect for brunch or a dinner party and you can prepare all of the elements in advance and just bake the pastry on the day.

SERVES 4-6

1 hour

INGREDIENTS

½ OZ (15 G)	Chives
9 OZ (250 G)	Vegan puff pastry sheet
—	Plant-based milk, for brushing
—	Ground black pepper
—	Lemon zest, to serve

FOR THE CASHEW TOFU CREAM CHEESE (SEE TIP)

1 CUP (120 G)	Cashews
11 OZ (320 G)	Medium-firm tofu
2-4 TBSP	Unsweetened plant-based milk
3 TBSP	Lemon juice
3 TBSP	Nutritional yeast
1½ TBSP	Apple cider vinegar (or more lemon juice)
1½ TSP	Garlic powder

FOR THE MARINATED CARROTS

2	Large carrots (about 11 oz/320 g)
1½ TSP	Olive oil
2 TBSP	Lemon juice
¾ TSP	Maple syrup
¾ TBSP	Tamari or light soy sauce

1. Preheat the oven to 400°F (200°C).

2. Tip the cashews for the cashew cream into a heatproof bowl. Pour over enough boiling water to cover, then set aside.

3. To make the carrots, bring a large pot of well-salted water to a boil and prepare a bowl of iced water.

4. Peel the carrots, then use the peeler to slice the carrots into thick ribbons. Add the carrot ribbons to the pot and boil for 2 minutes, then drain and dunk into the ice bath to stop the carrots cooking further. Gently toss the carrot ribbons in the ice water for a minute or so, then drain.

5. Combine the rest of the ingredients for the marinated carrots in a sealable container. Stir in 1½ tablespoons of water, then add the drained carrots and toss gently to combine with the marinade. Set aside for at least 20 minutes and up to 2 days to marinate.

6. Drain the cashews and tip into a high-speed blender or food processor. Add all the other cashew cream ingredients and blend until smooth. Add a little more plant-based milk if needed to help get it around the blender, but don't add too much, or it will become too runny. Taste and adjust the seasonings to your liking.

7. Finely chop the chives; this is easiest to do with scissors while they are still in a bunch. Stir three-quarters of them into the cashew cream, then store in the fridge until needed. Leftover cream can be stored in the fridge for 3–4 days.

¾ TSP	Rice vinegar
¼ TSP	Salt
¼ TSP	Freshly ground black pepper
¼ TSP	Liquid smoke or coconut aminos (optional, brings a smokiness)
¾	Nori sheet, torn
¾ TSP	Capers, plus ½ tsp brine
¾ TSP	Hot smoked paprika (or sweet smoked paprika, if you prefer)
¼ TSP	Garlic powder

FOR THE EVERYTHING BAGEL SEASONING

2½ TBSP	White sesame seeds
2 TBSP	Black sesame seeds
2 TSP	Onion powder
2 TSP	Garlic powder
2 TSP	Poppy seeds
3 TSP	Flaky sea salt

TIP

IF YOU DON'T HAVE TIME TO MAKE THE CASHEW CREAM, JUST STIR THE CHIVES INTO 6 OZ (160 G) VEGAN CREAM CHEESE.

8. To make the everything bagel seasoning, simply mix everything together in a jar and give it a good shake. This will make more than you need, so store any leftovers in a jar and use to scatter over toast, noodles, soups or roasted vegetables.

9. Next, bake the tart. Roll out the pastry sheet onto a baking sheet. Use a sharp knife to score a border about ¾ in (2 cm) in from the edges. Prick the inner area all over with a fork. Brush the edges with a little plant-based milk and generously sprinkle over the seasoning so that it covers the entire border of the pastry. Don't worry if you get some inside the border.

10. Bake for 12–15 minutes until lightly golden on top and perfectly baked and crispy underneath. Push down the middle, as it will puff up. Allow to cool slightly before assembling.

11. To assemble the tart, spread a generous layer of chive cream over the inner section of the pastry. Evenly layer the marinated carrots over the top. Finish with plenty of lemon zest, a good grinding of black pepper, some extra capers and the remaining finely chopped chives. Serve.

Dessert Spoon

I'm not a big baker, so when I need to satisfy my sweet tooth, I want something fairly simple to make, delicious, and not too sweet. Many of the recipes in this chapter are for quick and easy sweet treats (some of which are surprisingly healthy), while others are a little more involved and experimental, perfect for entertaining. One thing that I want to share is that you can indulge your sweet tooth at any time of the day – having your sweet things earlier in the day gives your body more time to use that energy up rather than right before bed. Cake for breakfast?

Chocolate Tart with Salted Oat Base

This is a dessert I've been making for years as my go-to when I have guests over. Perfect for a dinner party, but easy enough that you need no excuse for making it on a Wednesday evening just for yourself. Because most of the flavor comes from the chocolate, buy the best quality you can, as the tastier the chocolate, the better your tart will be. You'll need a 10 in (25 cm) tart pan with a loose base for this.

SERVES 8–12
40 minutes, plus 2 hours to set

INGREDIENTS

1¾ CUPS (170 G)	Oats (gluten-free if needed)
⅓ CUP (35 G)	Cacao powder
2 TBSP	Ground flaxseed
1¼ TBSP	Maple syrup
1½ TBSP	Tahini
¼ CUP (50 G)	Olive oil
1¼ TSP	Flaky sea salt
2 TBSP	Cacao nibs (optional)

FOR THE FILLING

1 LB (500 G)	Vegan dark chocolate (at least 70% cocoa)
1¼ CUPS (300 ML)	Coconut cream (or 2 × 14 oz/400 ml cans of full-fat coconut milk—see Tip)
2 TBSP	Maple syrup
2 TBSP	Espresso (or strongly brewed coffee)

TIP
YOU CAN USE COCONUT MILK INSTEAD OF COCONUT CREAM. REFRIGERATE THE CANS OVERNIGHT SO THAT THE CREAM SEPARATES FROM THE WATER IN THE CAN. SCOOP OUT THE THICK CREAM FROM THE TOP AND USE THE COCONUT WATER FOR SOMETHING ELSE.

1. Preheat the oven to 400°F (200°C) and line your tart pan with parchment paper.

2. Add the oats, cacao powder and ground flax to a food processor. Process into a fine powder. Then add 1 tablespoon water, along with the maple syrup, tahini, olive oil and salt, and blend again until combined.

3. Push the mixture evenly into the base and up the sides of the prepared pan. Bake for 10 minutes, then allow to cool completely.

4. To make the filling, prepare a bain-marie by placing a heatproof bowl over a pot of simmering water. Make sure the bottom of the bowl doesn't touch the hot water below.

5. Break the chocolate into small pieces and put them into the bowl. Add the coconut cream, maple syrup and espresso to the chocolate and stir until the chocolate has melted and everything has come together. Taste and adjust the sweetness if you like.

6. Quickly pour the mixture into the tart base. To help smooth out the top, gently tap the tart on the work surface and wiggle it from side to side to even out the filling.

7. Allow to cool, then put it in the fridge to set for at least 2 hours. Once it has set, sprinkle the cacao nibs (if using) over the tart, then slice and serve. The tart will keep for up to 5 days covered in the fridge.

• GLUTEN-FREE   • NUT-FREE

No-Bake Fudgy Chocolate Log (Doukissa)

Doukissa is a Cypriot and Greek favorite. It's a fridge cake made with melted chocolate and cookies, but also sometimes rum or dried fruit and nuts (a classic combo), so mix up the ingredients and make it your own. This is my vegan version of the classic, made richer and fudge-like with tahini.

SERVES 6-8
10 minutes, plus 1 hour to set

INGREDIENTS

7 OZ (200 G)	Vegan dark chocolate (at least 70% cocoa)
4	Digestive cookies (or 2 oz/60 g any other vegan cookie), plus extra to serve
2½ TBSP	Walnuts, plus extra to serve
⅔ CUP (170 G)	Tahini
2 TBSP	Maple syrup (agave or golden syrup works too)
⅓ TSP	Flaky sea salt
2 TSP	Vanilla extract (optional)
—	Zest of 1 orange

1. Line a medium-sized glass container or dish (or a baking sheet) with plastic wrap or parchment paper.

2. Prepare a bain-marie by placing a heatproof bowl over a pot of simmering water. Make sure the bottom of the bowl doesn't touch the hot water below. Break up the chocolate and add it to the bowl, stirring as it melts. If you prefer, you can melt it in a heatproof bowl in the microwave, heating it in 30-second bursts and stirring between each one.

3. Break up the cookies into small pieces and roughly chop the walnuts.

4. Transfer the melted chocolate into a large bowl, then add the tahini and maple syrup and stir well to combine. Add the nuts, cookies and salt, along with the vanilla extract, if using, and mix well, making sure everything is combined and evenly covered in chocolate.

5. Pour the chocolate mixture into the prepared dish and use the back of a spoon to even out the top. Place in the fridge for at least an hour to set.

6. Once set, use the plastic wrap or parchment paper to help you turn it out onto a serving platter. Garnish with some more crumbled nuts and cookies, and finish with a scattering of orange zest.

7. This will keep in the fridge in an airtight container for a week.

Fig & Granola Frozen Yogurt Pops

This is one of my favorite easy summer snacks. The recipe is completely customizable; you can roast any fruit that's about to go bad and mix it into the yogurt to help save on food waste. Use fruit that's in season for the best flavor. You'll need popsicle molds (see Tip).

SERVE 5-6

10 minutes, plus freezing time

INGREDIENTS

1¾ CUPS (400 G)	Vegan Greek-style yogurt
6–8 TBSP	Maple syrup (depending on your preference)
4–6	Ripe figs
3 TBSP	Vegan granola

TIP

IF YOU DON'T HAVE POPSICLE MOLDS, YOU CAN JUST USE SMALL WASHED-OUT YOGURT CONTAINERS, AND USE A TEASPOON AS THE STICK.

1. Pour the yogurt into a bowl and add the maple syrup to taste.

2. Slice the figs into thin rounds.

3. Tip a little granola into the bottom of each popsicle mold, then add the fig slices. Try to push them to the edges of the mold so they don't get covered with yogurt. Now carefully spoon the yogurt carefully into the molds, trying not to dislodge the figs. Add a little more granola on top, but make sure to push it into the yogurt so that it has something to stick to.

4. Insert the sticks and freeze for at least 3 hours until set.

Fudgy Tahini Brownies

These are everything you could ask for in a brownie; fudgy, chocolatey, gooey and rich. The tahini caramel is an added bonus that takes it to the next level. Make a bit extra and drizzle it over your morning oats, ice cream or onto toast.

SERVES 12
1 hour

INGREDIENTS

½ CUP (120 ML)	Almond milk
1 CUP (180 G)	Granulated sugar
½ TSP	Vanilla extract
6 OZ (180 G)	Vegan dark chocolate (at least 70% cocoa)
4½ TBSP (65 G)	Vegan butter
4 TBSP	Tahini
1 CUP (135 G)	All-purpose flour
½ CUP (45 G)	Cacao powder
⅓ TSP	Flaky sea salt, plus extra to serve (optional)
½ TSP	Baking powder
1 TBSP	Sesame seeds

FOR THE TAHINI CARAMEL

2½ TBSP	Tahini
2½ TBSP	Maple syrup or agave
2 TSP	Date syrup (or use more maple syrup)

1. Preheat the oven to 350°F (180°C) and line an 8 × 11 in (20 × 28 cm) baking pan with parchment paper.

2. Combine the almond milk and sugar in a small saucepan and place over low heat for about 5 minutes until the sugar melts. Allow to cool slightly, then stir through the vanilla extract.

3. Prepare a bain-marie by placing a heatproof bowl over a pot of simmering water. Make sure the bottom of the bowl doesn't touch the hot water below. Break up the chocolate and add it to the bowl, along with the vegan butter and tahini. Stir to melt together, then set aside to cool slightly until just warm.

4. Pour the sugar and almond mixture into the chocolate mixture and whisk to combine.

5. Sift the flour and cacao powder into a large mixing bowl. Add the salt and baking powder, and stir to combine.

6. Add the chocolate mixture to the dry ingredients and stir with a spatula to combine.

7. Transfer the batter into the prepared baking pan and bake for 25–30 minutes. Don't over-bake, as the brownies will firm up as they cool. Allow to sit in the pan for 10 minutes, then turn out onto a wire rack to cool completely.

8. To make the tahini caramel, combine all the ingredients in a bowl and stir to combine.

9. Drizzle the tahini caramel over the brownie and top with a sprinkle of sesame seeds. Finish with a sprinkle of flaky sea salt, if you like. Store in an airtight container for up to 4 days.

Filo Cake with Orange & Yogurt (Soufra)

Soufra is a Greek filo dish that can be sweet or savory. The sweet version is made with buttered filo pastry and filled with a sweet custard. I've used soy yogurt for the creamy filling, which is baked between the crispy pastry swirls for a decadent and light dessert. You'll need a large 11–12 in (28–31 cm) shallow Dutch oven, casserole dish, cake pan or tart pan. If you only have a smaller vessel, you can use fewer filo sheets and less filling as needed.

SERVES 8–10
1 hour 15 minutes

INGREDIENTS

4 TBSP	Vegan butter or olive oil, for brushing
9½ OZ (270 G)	Filo pastry
⅓ CUP (30 G)	Sliced almonds
—	Maple syrup or confectioners' sugar, to finish (optional)

FOR THE FILLING

—	Zest and juice of 3 large oranges
1¾ CUPS (450 G)	Plain soy yogurt
¼ CUP (60 ML)	Olive oil
¾ CUP (160 G)	White sugar
½ TBSP	Cornstarch
½ TSP	Baking powder

1. Preheat the oven to 400°F (200°C).

2. Melt the butter, if using. Brush a large round baking dish or cake pan all over with the melted butter or olive oil.

3. Lay out one filo sheet and keep the rest covered with a slightly damp clean tea towel to stop them drying out. Brush a filo sheet with olive oil or butter and lay it flat in the baking dish. Brush another sheet and lay it diagonally over the first one, to cover the whole surface of the baking dish with the excess hanging over the sides. (Depending on the size of your sheets, you may need to repeat until the base is covered; you want just two layers of the sheets, covering the whole base.)

4. Brush another sheet and use your fingers to gently pull the two longest sides towards each other, scrunching them carefully, so you end up with a long, narrow piece, almost like a concertina. Coil it into a very loose rose (don't make it too tight or it won't cook properly) and place it in the center of the baking dish. Repeat with the remaining pastry sheets, wrapping them loosely around the central "rose" until you have filled the dish, making sure it's not too tight and there is plenty of space in between the folds. Fold any overhanging pastry (from the very first layer of sheets on the bottom) into the dish and scrunch it gently into the sides of the pastry coils.

5. Use the remaining oil or butter to brush the top of the pastry. Bake for 15–18 minutes on the middle rack until golden brown all over.

CONTINUED OVERLEAF

RECIPE CONTINUED

6   Meanwhile, make the filling. Measure out ⅔ cup (150 ml) of orange juice from your oranges and add this to a bowl with the two-thirds of the orange zest. Add the yogurt, olive oil, sugar, cornstarch and baking powder, and whisk to combine.

7   When the filo has had its first bake, reduce the oven temperature to 350°F (180°C). Carefully and slowly pour the yogurt filling into the filo, getting it into all of the cracks as evenly as possible. Sprinkle the sliced almonds over the top, breaking some up into crumbles. Bake for 25 minutes on the middle rack.

8   Remove from the oven and scatter the remaining orange zest over the top. Add a drizzle of maple syrup or a dusting of confectioners' sugar if you like your desserts quite sweet. Let it cool for at least 10 minutes before serving. Store in an airtight container for up to 5 days.

Roasted Pears with Chai Custard

This is the ideal dessert if you are looking for something easy to make, light to eat and not too sweet. The pears are roasted, giving them an extra depth of flavor and the warmth of the chai custard is lifted by the orange zest so everything comes together in one perfect bite.

SERVES 4
1 hour 10 minutes

FOR THE PEARS

6	Small, underripe pears (or 4 large ones)
3½ TBSP (50 G)	Vegan butter
¼ CUP (60 ML)	Maple syrup, plus extra to serve
½	Lemon

FOR THE SPICE MIX (SEE TIP)

1 TSP	Ground ginger
¼ TSP	Ground cardamom
⅛ TSP	Ground nutmeg
—	Pinch of ground cloves
10	Twists of black pepper

FOR THE CHAI CUSTARD

4¼ CUPS (1 LITER)	Almond milk (or use soy milk, or oat milk if not gluten-free)
½ CUP (110 G)	White sugar
1 TSP	Vanilla extract (optional)
½ CUP (60 G)	Cornstarch

FOR THE ORANGE PINE NUT CRUMBS

½ CUP (60 G)	Pine nuts
—	Zest of 1 orange

TIP
YOU CAN SUBSTITUTE THE SPICE MIX FOR 7 CHAI TEABAGS. ADD THESE TO A PAN WITH THE MILK AND STEEP AT A GENTLE SIMMER FOR 15 MINUTES. REMOVE THE TEABAGS, THEN ADD THE SUGAR AND VANILLA AND PROCEED AS ABOVE.

1. Preheat the oven to 350°F (180°C).

2. Peel the pears and slice in half. Remove the cores with a small measuring spoon or melon baller (or a knife).

3. Melt the butter in a pot over low heat. Add the maple syrup and squeeze in the lemon half, then whisk to combine. Add the pears and toss to coat, then tip into a small oven dish, sprinkling with 2 tablespoons of water. Nestle the squeezed lemon half in with the pears. The pears should fit snugly into the dish without too much space around them, so if you need to, move them to a smaller dish—they will shrink as they cook.

4. Bake for 40–60 minutes (depending on ripeness) until soft and starting to brown. Turn them once or twice and baste with the juices. Check they are done by piercing them with a sharp knife.

5. Meanwhile, make the custard. First, mix the spice mix ingredients in a small bowl. Combine the spice mix with the milk, sugar and vanilla, if using, in a saucepan. Sift in the cornstarch (don't skip sifting, as you may end up with a lumpy custard). Whisk well to combine, then place over low-medium heat. Gently simmer, whisking continuously with a metal whisk, for 4–5 minutes until it has thickened. Keep in mind that it will thicken further as it cools. If you end up with lumps, put the mixture into a blender and blend until smooth. If it is too thick, whisk in a little more milk.

6. To make the pine nut crumbs, lightly toast the pine nuts in a dry frying pan over medium heat for about 3 minutes until just golden. Bash them gently using a mortar and pestle and return them to the hot pan to toast for another 2 minutes or so. Stir often and don't leave them, as pine nuts can burn very quickly. Remove from the heat and put them back in the mortar, add the orange zest and bash gently to release its flavor.

7. To serve, pour a ladleful of custard into each bowl. Add 2 large or 3 small pear halves to each, and top with a tablespoon of the pine nut crumb. Finish with a drizzle of maple syrup, if you like.

● GLUTEN-FREE

Kalamata Cookie Ice-Cream Sandwich

If you like the combination of salty and sweet, then this olive cookie will be your new favorite treat. These cookies are so simple to make and are the perfect balance between crumbly, soft and moist. The kalamata olives bring an unexpected depth of flavor that works so well with the sugary coating. Having two cookies with some ice cream in between turns them into a nostalgic, deliciously decadent treat.

SERVES 6
35 minutes

INGREDIENTS

2 TBSP	Ground flaxseed
5 OZ (140 G)	Kalamata olives
3¼ CUPS (400 G)	All-purpose flour
—	Zest of 2 lemons
1 TSP	Baking powder
⅔ CUP (140 G)	Sugar or soft light brown sugar
½ CUP (120 ML)	Extra virgin olive oil
6	Scoops of vegan vanilla ice cream

1. Preheat the oven to 410°F (210°C) and line a baking sheet with parchment paper.

2. Add the ground flaxseed to a small bowl with 6 tablespoons of water. Set aside for 5 minutes.

3. Pit and roughly chop the olives.

4. Add the flour, lemon zest, olives, ground flaxseed, baking powder and ½ cup (100 g) of the sugar and stir to combine. Add the olive oil and mix well. I like to use my hands here to crumble the mixture together.

5. Scoop out about a tablespoon of the batter and roll into a ball. Repeat with the remaining batter. You should end up with 12 evenly sized balls, so redistribute the dough if needed.

6. Pour the remaining sugar into a small bowl and roll each ball around the bowl to cover in sugar. Place the balls on the prepared baking sheet and push them down gently with your fingers to flatten until about ½ in (1.5 cm) thick.

7. Bake for 15 minutes, then remove from the oven and allow to cool completely on a wire rack. Place a large container in your freezer.

8. Once completely cooled, add a scoop of slightly softened ice cream to the underside of one cookie. Use the back of a spoon to flatten the ice cream a little. Add another cookie on top and push down gently to help them stick together. Pop each finished ice-cream sandwich into the container in the freezer so they don't melt while you prepare the rest, then serve.

Mocha Mess

This is a play on a British Eton mess, but with the coffee and chocolate flavors of mocha. The chocolate almond drizzle is an upgraded version of that chocolate hazelnut spread we all know, and the coffee cream gives it a real adult twist. Making meringues out of aquafaba is a bit of magic and makes this a really special dessert that's deceptively simple to make.

SERVES 4–6
2 hours 30 minutes

FOR THE MERINGUES
- 14 OZ (400 G) Can of chickpeas
- ½ TSP Cream of tartar
- 2⅔ CUPS (300 G) Confectioners' sugar
- 1 TSP Vanilla extract

FOR THE COFFEE CREAM
- ⅔ CUP (160 ML) Coconut cream (or 1 × 14 oz/400 ml can of coconut milk—see Tip on page 202)
- 1 TSP Vanilla extract
- ⅓ CUP (45 G) Confectioners' sugar
- 2 TSP Strongly brewed coffee or espresso

FOR THE CHOCOLATE ALMOND DRIZZLE
- 1¾ OZ (50 G) Vegan dark chocolate (at least 70% cocoa)
- 1¾ TBSP Almond butter (or use hazelnut butter)
- — Sweetener of choice (optional)

FOR THE TOPPING
- 2½ CUPS (300 G) Raspberries

TIP
THE MERINGUES WILL KEEP IN AN AIRTIGHT CONTAINER FOR UP TO 2 WEEKS. STORE THE CHOCOLATE ALMOND DRIZZLE IN A SEALED JAR IN THE FRIDGE FOR UP TO 1 WEEK. STORE COFFEE CREAM SEPARATELY IN AN AIRTIGHT CONTAINER IN THE FRIDGE FOR UP TO 3 DAYS.

1. Preheat the oven to 250°F (120°C). Line a baking sheet with parchment paper.

2. To make the meringues, drain the chickpeas and measure out ½ cup (120 ml) of the liquid (aquafaba). Keep the chickpeas to use in another recipe. Pour the liquid into a bowl and add the cream of tartar. Beat using a handheld electric mixer or stand mixer until soft peaks form. Gradually add the confectioners' sugar, 1 tablespoon at a time, beating continually, for about 10 minutes until glossy peaks form. Beat in the vanilla extract until well incorporated.

3. Spoon the meringue mixture into small circles on the prepared baking sheet and bake for about 90 minutes until the meringues are firm and come away easily from the paper. Turn off the oven and leave the meringues inside to cool slowly and completely.

4. Meanwhile, make the coffee cream. Put the coconut cream, vanilla, confectioners' sugar and cooled coffee into a mixing bowl and beat with an electric mixer for about 5 minutes until combined and creamy.

5. To make the almond chocolate drizzle, prepare a bain-marie by placing a heatproof bowl over a pot of simmering water. Make sure the water doesn't touch the bottom of the bowl. Break up the chocolate and add it to the bowl, stirring until melted, then remove from the heat. If you prefer, you can melt it in a heatproof bowl in the microwave, heating it in 30-second bursts and stirring between each one.

6. Add the nut butter to the melted chocolate and taste, adding a little confectioners' sugar, agave or maple syrup to sweeten, if you like.

7. To assemble, spoon the coffee cream into bowls, crumble a couple of meringues into each and drizzle over the chocolate nut drizzle. Finish with plenty of raspberries.

Banana Tahini Ice Cream with Pecan Caramel Crumbles

This is the ultimate ice cream, served with all the trimmings. You won't believe that it's a sugar-free, healthy version of your favorite tub and I have no issues eating this for breakfast on a hot day. You'll need to freeze the bananas overnight before you start.

SERVES 8–10
15 minutes, plus freezing time

INGREDIENTS

5	Ripe bananas
14 OZ (400 ML)	Can of full-fat coconut milk
1 CUP (100 G)	Pecans
3 OZ (80 G)	Pitted dates
–	Pinch of salt
3 TBSP	Maple syrup or agave, plus extra to taste
1 TBSP	Tahini
1 TBSP	Vodka (optional —see Tips)
1 TBSP	Date syrup

TIPS

IF YOU DON'T HAVE A SMALL HIGH-SPEED FOOD PROCESSOR, YOU MIGHT HAVE A HARD TIME WITH THE PECAN CARAMEL. A GOOD ALTERNATIVE IS TO BLEND SOFTENED DATES OR DATE PASTE WITH NUT BUTTER FOR A SIMILAR RESULT.

THE VODKA IS TASTELESS—IT HELPS PREVENT ICE CRYSTALS FORMING, WHICH GIVES A SMOOTHER, CREAMIER ICE CREAM, BUT YOU CAN LEAVE IT OUT IF YOU PREFER.

1. Peel the bananas, chop into small pieces and freeze overnight. Place the can of coconut milk in the fridge overnight too.

2. The next day, preheat the oven to 400°F (200°C). Scatter the pecans over a baking sheet and roast for 5–8 minutes until golden. Reserve a small handful for the topping.

3. If your dates are very hard, soak them for 5 minutes in a bowl of hot water, then drain and squeeze out the water.

4. Add the dates, pecans and a pinch of salt to a small food processor and blend until combined. It will be a chunky mix, not smooth, but it just needs to come together enough to roll into little balls. Taste and add a little agave or maple syrup if you like.

5. When you are ready to make the ice cream, carefully scoop out the cream that has solidified at the top of the coconut milk can (keep the remaining liquid to use in a smoothie), and place into a high-speed food processor or large blender. Then add the frozen bananas, maple syrup or agave, tahini and vodka, if using. Blend until just smooth. Take care not to over-blend; you are aiming for a soft-serve consistency. Taste and see if you would like more maple syrup, and adjust to your liking.

6. Pour the mixture into a plastic tub or loaf pan and tear off small pieces of the pecan caramel, stirring them into the ice cream mixture. Add as much as you like. If you have some left over, you can roll the mixture into balls and freeze or refrigerate to enjoy as a snack.

7. Drizzle the date syrup over the ice cream. Chop the reserved pecans and scatter over the top.

8. Freeze for at least 3 hours and allow to thaw for at least 10 minutes before serving.

● GLUTEN-FREE   ● REFINED SUGAR-FREE

Peanut Butter Cherry Jam Semifreddo

Something in between an ice-cream cake (semifreddo) and a "cheesecake," this is the ultimate dessert to impress. This recipe makes a big cake, which you can slice into pieces and store in the freezer, taking a piece out whenever you fancy one, as it keeps for months.

SERVES 10
30 minutes, plus 4 hours to set

FOR THE BASE

1 TBSP	Coconut oil
1 CUP (170 G)	Pitted dates
1 CUP (100 G)	Almonds (or any other nut)
¾ CUP (80 G)	Oats (gluten-free if needed)
1 TSP	Agave
–	Pinch of salt

FOR THE FILLING

4 CUPS (450 G)	Cashews
2 TBSP (25 G)	Coconut oil
1 CUP (240 ML)	Full-fat coconut milk (from a can)
½–⅔ CUP (120–150 ML)	Agave
3½ TBSP	Smooth peanut butter

FOR THE TOPPING

⅓ CUP (100 G)	Cherry jam
2 TBSP	Roasted peanuts

TIPS

YOU CAN SLICE THE CAKE INTO PIECES AND KEEP THESE IN A SEALED CONTAINER IN THE FREEZER FOR UP TO 3 MONTHS.

FEEL FREE TO SWAP THE CHERRY JAM FOR ANOTHER JAM. YOU COULD EVEN PLAY AROUND WITH DIFFERENT NUT BUTTERS LIKE ALMOND OR HAZELNUT.

1. Line the base of a 10–11 in (25–28 cm) cake pan with parchment paper.

2. Place the cashews for the filling in a big bowl and pour over plenty of boiling water. Leave to soak for at least 2 hours or overnight. If you don't have a powerful food processor, do this the night before to get the cashews as soft as possible.

3. Start by making the base. If the coconut oil is solid, melt it in the microwave or by placing the jar in a bowl of hot water.

4. Combine the dates, almonds and oats in a food processor, along with the coconut oil, agave and a pinch of salt. Pulse until it comes together in even crumbs. It should come into a ball if you squeeze in your hand.

5. Pour the date and nut mixture into the prepared pan and spread it out as evenly as you can with your hands. Take a scrap of parchment paper and a glass with a flat base. Lay the parchment paper under the glass and use it to push down on the mixture so that it is evenly spread. You can use the back of a spoon to press down the edges. Set aside.

6. Next, make the filling. Drain and rinse the cashews and wash out the food processor. Add the cashews to the food processor, along with the coconut oil, coconut milk, agave and peanut butter. Blend until very smooth. If your food processor is not powerful or sharp enough and you have a high-speed blender, you can use that instead.

7. Pour this mixture into the cake pan. Add big dollops of cherry jam all over the top and use a knife to gently swirl it into the creamy mixture. To get it smooth on the top, gently tap the pan on the counter a few times. Sprinkle over the roasted peanuts.

8. Cover the pan with plastic wrap or a plate and place in the freezer to set. It will need at least 4 hours to fully set. Remove it from the freezer to thaw about 25 minutes before serving.

● GLUTEN-FREE ● REFINED SUGAR-FREE

Spiced Chile Chocolate Mousse

These flavors are inspired by Mayan hot chocolate, an ancient cacao drink. The chile gives a kick and the cinnamon and cardamom are warming and complementary to the dark chocolate. If you're not feeling brave enough for the spices, feel free to skip them for a more traditional, sweet chocolate flavor, as this really is all about the light, airy mousse.

SERVES 4–5

30 minutes, plus 1 hour to set

INGREDIENTS

1 TSP	Ancho chile (or use ½ tsp mild cayenne pepper)
14 OZ (400 G)	Can of chickpeas
1 TSP	Lemon juice
7 OZ (200 G)	Vegan dark chocolate (at least 70% cocoa)
¼ TSP	Ground cinnamon
¼ TSP	Ground cardamom
1 TBSP	Strongly brewed coffee
–	Pinch of salt
3 TBSP	Agave or maple syrup

TO SERVE (OPTIONAL)

–	Vegan whipped cream
–	Berries
–	Dark chocolate shavings
–	Pinch of chile powder

1. Remove any seeds from the ancho chile and place in a hot, dry frying pan over medium-low heat. Toast for about 2 minutes on each side until blackened in places and fragrant.

2. Grind the toasted chile in a spice grinder or small high-speed blender. Make sure it's completely ground into a very fine powder. Measure out 2 teaspoons of the powder. (Skip these steps if using cayenne pepper.)

3. Drain the chickpeas and measure out ¾ cup (175 ml) of the liquid (aquafaba). Keep the chickpeas to use in another recipe. Add the aquafaba and lemon juice to a mixing bowl and whisk with a handheld electric mixer or stand mixer for 10 minutes, until stiff peaks form. The mixture should be 8–10 times its original volume.

4. Meanwhile, prepare a bain-marie by placing a heatproof bowl over a pot of simmering water. Make sure the bottom of the bowl doesn't touch the hot water below. Chop the chocolate and add it to the bowl, stirring as it melts. Once about two-thirds of the chocolate has melted, remove from the heat and stir to allow the residual heat to melt the rest. If you prefer, you can melt it in a heatproof bowl in the microwave, heating it in 30-second bursts and stirring between each one.

5. Gently fold about one third of the whipped aquafaba into the melted chocolate, then stir in the chile, cinnamon, cardamom, coffee, salt and agave until fully combined.

6. Carefully and slowly pour the melted chocolate mix into the rest of the whipped aquafaba. It will reduce, but stir gently enough to just incorporate the chocolate without pushing out the air.

7. Once fully incorporated, spoon the mousse into cups or small ramekins and leave in the fridge for an hour to set. Serve topped with vegan whipped cream, berries or shaved chocolate, and a sprinkle of chile if you like.

● GLUTEN-FREE   ● NUT-FREE

Sumac & Pomegranate Cherries on Buckwheat Crêpes

Buckwheat flour is a great, nutrient-dense swap for refined wholewheat flour. It's the main ingredient in a French galette and is loved for its strong, nutty flavor, but mixing it with all-purpose flour balances the strong flavor in these crêpes. They're perfect for brunch, or as a late-night treat.

MAKES 4–6 CRÊPES
1 hour

INGREDIENTS

1 CUP (120 G)	Buckwheat flour
⅔ CUP (80 G)	All-purpose flour (or swap for gluten-free)
¾–2 CUPS (400–450 ML)	Unsweetened plant-based milk (gluten-free if needed)
¼ TSP	Salt
2½–4 TBSP	White sugar (to taste)
2–3 TBSP	Vegan butter or coconut oil

FOR THE CHERRIES

4 CUPS (500 G)	Cherries (fresh or frozen)
3 TSP	White or brown sugar
1 TSP	Pomegranate molasses
½ TSP	Sumac
—	Juice of 1 lemon, plus extra to serve

FOR THE CHOCOLATE SAUCE

5½ OZ (150 G)	Vegan dark chocolate
2 TBSP	Plant-based milk (gluten-free if needed)

TO SERVE

—	Toasted nuts, such as pistachios, almonds or hazelnuts
⅓ CUP (100 G)	Soy yogurt
—	Maple syrup (optional)

1. To make the cherries, add the cherries, sugar, pomegranate molasses and 2 tablespoons of water to a small saucepan. Simmer over low heat for 10 minutes for frozen cherries or 15 minutes for fresh cherries, until just softened. Remove the cherries using a slotted spoon and set aside in a bowl. Add the sumac to the liquid in the pan and continue to heat for another 5 minutes to reduce the liquid until you have a syrupy consistency. Stir in the lemon juice.

2. To make the crêpes, whisk together the flours, 1⅔ cups (400 ml) milk, salt and sugar. The batter should be fairly thin; add a little more milk as needed. Heat about ½ teaspoon of the vegan butter or coconut oil in a large frying pan over medium heat. When the pan is hot and the butter/oil is melted, take the pan off the heat and pour in a ladle of the crêpe batter. Quickly swirl it around the pan to get a thin, even crêpe. Return to the heat and cook for about 3 minutes, until the sides are peeling away from the pan and the crêpe is cooked enough to flip. Carefully flip it and cook for another 2 minutes. Set aside on a plate to keep warm. Continue with the rest of the batter.

3. To make the chocolate sauce, break the chocolate into small pieces. You can either melt it in the microwave or in a bain-marie. To melt in the microwave, place the chocolate in a bowl with the plant milk and microwave, stirring at 30-second intervals, until melted. To make a bain-marie, place the chocolate and milk in a heatproof bowl and set it over pot of simmering water. Stir often until the heat has melted the chocolate.

4. Roughly chop the toasted nuts.

5. To serve, lay two or three crêpes on a plate, add a few tablespoons of soy yogurt, then top with the cherries and cherry syrup. Drizzle over the melted chocolate and scatter over the nuts. Finish with a squeeze of lemon and a drizzle of maple syrup, if you like.

Ultimate Vegan French Toast

French toast needs no introduction. This is my tried, tested and well-loved vegan version, with a little added protein sneaked in to help keep you full, and layers of flavor piled on.

SERVES 2
30 minutes

INGREDIENTS

5½ OZ (150 G)	Silken tofu
4 TBSP	Soft dark brown sugar
1½ TBSP	Chickpea flour
⅔ CUP (150 ML)	Soy milk
½ TSP	Vanilla extract
⅛ TSP	Ground nutmeg
1 TSP	Ground cinnamon
4	Thickly cut slices of soft white bread
4 TBSP	Vegan butter

TO SERVE

½ CUP (150 G)	Almond butter (or use peanut butter or tahini)
—	Maple syrup
—	Raspberries
—	Pistachios
—	Soy yogurt

TIP

EXPERIMENT WITH DIFFERENT TOPPINGS TO FIND YOUR FAVORITE COMBINATION. I ALSO LOVE SLICED BANANA WITH CINNAMON AND MAPLE SYRUP, STRAWBERRIES AND MELTED CHOCOLATE, OR ICE CREAM WITH TAHINI CARAMEL IF YOU'RE FEELING EXTRA INDULGENT.

1. In a high-speed blender, combine the tofu, brown sugar, chickpea flour, soy milk, vanilla, nutmeg and cinnamon. Blend until completely smooth. Pour the mixture into a wide, shallow bowl or a small baking sheet.

2. Place a slice of bread into the mixture and soak each side for 30 seconds, until fully drenched in the liquid. Remove and repeat with the remaining bread slices.

3. Heat a frying pan over low-medium heat. Add 1 tablespoon of the vegan butter and, when it's almost melted, add a slice of toast and increase the heat to medium. Don't try to move the toast until at least 2 minutes have passed, as you will break the crust that is forming. Check after 2 minutes; if it has slightly charred edges and has a golden crust, it's done. When it's done, flip and cook one the other side. Repeat with each slice.

4. To serve, spread each slice with almond butter, top with maple syrup, raspberries, pistachios and a spoonful of soy yogurt.

Vanilla Pudding with Miso Caramel

If you are not familiar with agar agar, it's a vegan alternative to gelatine. It's easy to find online, not too expensive and a little goes a long way, so I really suggest giving it a try. This simple dessert is creamy and light, and you can use it as a base for your favorite flavors, like berries or matcha. This one has a Japanese and Szechuanese twist, which is a bit daring, but decadent and delicious.

SERVES 4
25 minutes, plus 2 hours to set

INGREDIENTS

FOR THE VANILLA PUDDINGS

—	Neutral oil, for greasing
1 LB 5 OZ (600 G)	Silken tofu
2 TSP	Vanilla extract
4 TSP	Agar agar powder
2 TBSP	Lemon juice
5 TBSP	Maple syrup

FOR THE MISO CARAMEL SAUCE

1 CUP (180 G)	Light brown sugar
½ CUP (120 ML)	Coconut milk
3½ TSP	Miso paste
2 TSP	Vegan butter (nut-free if needed)
—	Salt

FOR THE SZECHUAN SESAME CRUMBS

2 TSP	Szechuan peppercorns
4 TSP	Toasted sesame seeds

TIP
FEEL FREE TO SWAP OUT THE SZECHUAN PEPPERCORNS FOR MORE SESAME SEEDS IF YOU LIKE.

1. Wipe the insides of four ramekins with a little neutral oil. This will help the puddings slip out later.

2. Combine all the ingredients for the puddings in a blender and blend until smooth. Taste for sweetness and add a little more maple syrup if you like (up to 1 tablespoon).

3. Pour the mixture into a small pot and heat over a steady, medium-low heat for exactly 8 minutes, stirring often to make sure it doesn't boil. The time is important as it won't set if it doesn't cook for long enough and it might be too hard if it cooks for too long. After 8 minutes, pour into the prepared ramekins and place in the fridge for 2 hours until set.

4. For the miso caramel sauce, combine the sugar with 3½ tablespoons of water in a pot and stir to combine. Place over low heat and melt, swirling the pan occasionally, for 6–8 minutes, or until the sugar has dissolved and it all starts to bubble gently.

5. In a small bowl, whisk the coconut milk, miso, butter and salt until smooth. Pour into a separate small pot and place over low heat, gently warming through to help the ingredients combine. Slowly add this mixture to the caramel pot, whisking quickly between each addition. The mixture will bubble, so be careful. Allow to cool before pouring into a glass jar or container.

6. Next, make the sesame crumbs. Lightly toast the Szechuan peppercorns in a dry frying pan over medium heat for 3–4 minutes, then crush in a mortar and pestle to release the shells. Use a sieve to sift out the shells and discard them. In a bowl, combine the sesame seeds with the crushed peppercorns.

7. To serve, turn each ramekin over onto a plate or bowl. The puddings should slip out easily, but if not, gently insert a knife into the side of the ramekin to coax it out. Pour some miso caramel over or around the puddings, and sprinkle the sesame crumbs on top, then enjoy.

● GLUTEN-FREE ● NUT-FREE

Little
Jars

Great condiments can make your cooking so much easier, quicker, and more flavorful. A drizzle of this and a sprinkle of that can turn a basic meal into a memorable one. Having a good selection of condiments is your secret weapon in the kitchen, including hot sauces and chile oils, mustards, miso, vegan mayonnaise, nuts, nutritional yeast and pickles. This chapter will start you off, with a select few of my favorite combinations to add extra umami, crunch, nutrition, flavor and texture to your meals.

1. Greek-Style Vinaigrette
2. Porcini Furikake
3. Lemon & Herb Seed Parm Sprinkle
4. Roasted Cashew Butter Drizzle
5. Dukkah
6. Savory Seed Granola
7. Aromatic Hot Agave
8. Hot & Sweet Beet Tahini Sauce

Greek-Style Vinaigrette

This is my go-to vinaigrette. I love to make a big batch, since it keeps in the fridge for about a week. It also makes a lovely marinade for roasted cabbage or tofu.

MAKES ENOUGH TO DRESS 2–4 SALADS
5 minutes

INGREDIENTS

1	Garlic clove or ½ tsp garlic powder
½ CUP (120 ML)	Olive oil
3 TBSP	Red wine vinegar (or sherry vinegar or muscatel vinegar)
1 TSP	Dried oregano
1 TSP	Dried basil
¼ TSP	Salt
1 TSP	Dijon mustard
5–8	Twists of black pepper
1 TSP	Agave (optional)

1. If you're using a fresh garlic clove, mince it, then add it to a jar with the rest of the ingredients. Seal the jar and shake well. Taste and adjust the seasonings as you like.

2. This will keep in a sealed jar in the fridge for up to a week.

GLUTEN-FREE   NUT-FREE

Porcini Furikake

Furikake is a traditional Japanese rice seasoning. It's usually made with fish flakes, but there are many flavors and variations. To bump up the umami, I've added porcini mushrooms and onion powder, which are not traditional. This addictive sprinkle is delicious on noodles, rice dishes, popcorn, soups and so much more.

MAKES ABOUT 20 SERVINGS
5 minutes

INGREDIENTS

3	Large nori sheets (for sushi)
½–1 TSP	Chile flakes (optional)
1 TBSP	Toasted sesame seeds
1 TSP	Porcini powder (or dried porcinis—see Tip)
1 TSP	Salt
1 TSP	White sugar
1¼ TSP	Onion powder

TIPS

THIS IS GREAT WITH OR WITHOUT CHILE FLAKES. THE AMOUNT I USE MAKES IT QUITE SPICY, SO IF YOU AREN'T SURE, LEAVE THEM OUT—YOU CAN ALWAYS ADD SOME AT THE END.

IF USING DRIED WHOLE PORCINIS INSTEAD OF PORCINI POWDER, PULSE TO A FINE POWDER FIRST.

1. Break up the nori sheets and add to a high-speed blender or spice grinder. Add the chile flakes, if using, and pulse until the nori sheets have turned into small flakes (not quite a powder).

2. Tip this mixture into a small jar. Add the rest of the ingredients and give it a good shake.

3. This will keep in a well-sealed jar for a few months.

Lemon & Herb Seed Parm Sprinkle

I always have a variation of this sprinkle on hand and add some to pastas, bakes, soups or wherever I want to give a boost of flavor, texture and a "cheesy" element. It's really delicious and also packs a nutritional punch thanks to the protein in the nutritional yeast and seeds.

MAKES 20 SERVINGS
5 minutes

INGREDIENTS

1 CUP (150 G)	Sunflower seeds (see Tip)
4 TBSP	Nutritional yeast
2 TSP	Dried mixed herbs (such as basil, thyme, dill, marjoram, parsley, sage or oregano)
1 TBSP	Sesame seeds
1½ TSP	Flaky sea salt, or 1 tsp fine sea salt
10	Twists of black pepper
—	Zest of 1 lemon
½ TSP	Garlic powder

TIP
YOU CAN SWAP THE SUNFLOWER SEEDS FOR RAW CASHEWS, SLICED ALMONDS, WALNUTS OR HEMP SEEDS.

1. Combine all the ingredients in a small food processor and pulse to a fine powder.

2. Store in an airtight container for up to a month.

● GLUTEN-FREE ● NUT-FREE

Roasted Cashew Butter Drizzle

This is a real flavor-bomb, and just a teaspoon will elevate any simple meal—drizzle it over roasted veggies, stir-fries and veggie rice bowls, or stir through blended beans to make a creamy pasta sauce, or into soups to make them thick and creamy with an added umami element. It might not seem like much, but it is lick-the-spoon good.

MAKES 5-8 SERVINGS
20 minutes

INGREDIENTS

- 1½ CUPS (175 G) Cashews
- ½ TBSP Miso paste
- 1¼ TSP Light soy sauce (or tamari if gluten-free)
- 2 TSP Apple cider vinegar
- 1¼ TSP Nutritional yeast

1. Preheat the oven to 400°F (200°C).

2. Tip the cashews onto a large roasting pan and roast for 7–8 minutes until golden, tossing halfway.

3. While still hot, add the cashews to a high-speed food processor and blend until a smooth nut butter forms. This will take about 10 minutes (or more). Keep scraping down the sides and keep blending, even when you think it's smooth enough. The more you blend, the more fats are released, and the creamier the nut butter will become. Add the miso right at the end and blend again to combine.

4. Add the rest of the ingredients, along with 6 tablespoons of water. Blend until smooth. At this consistency, it's perfect for drizzling over roasted veggies or spooning into soup. If you want to use it as a salad dressing, add another tablespoon of water and taste. You may want to add a little more of the other ingredients to make up for watering it down slightly.

5. This will keep in a sealed jar in the fridge for up to a week.

● GLUTEN-FREE ● ALLIUM-FREE

Dukkah

Dukkah is an Egyptian and Middle Eastern condiment made with variations of roasted nuts and seeds. It's fragrant, rich and aromatic, and is surprisingly good on almost everything. From ice cream and smoothie bowls to salads and roasted veg to sweet or savory oats, a sprinkle over whatever you're eating will add a nutty, earthy flavor and a lovely crunch. This is my favorite combination, but feel free to experiment with the ratios and swap out some of the nuts and seeds to make it your own. This makes a big batch, which you will get through in no time, but feel free to halve it if you like.

MAKES ABOUT 20-30 SERVINGS
15 minutes

INGREDIENTS

1 CUP (130 G)	Hazelnuts
½ CUP (70 G)	Almonds
1¼ CUPS (150 G)	Pistachios
⅓ CUP (50 G)	White sesame seeds
1 TBSP	Coriander seeds
1 TBSP	Fennel seeds
1 TSP	Cumin seeds
½ TBSP	Flaky sea salt
½–1 TSP	Aleppo pepper or chile flakes (optional)

1. Preheat the oven to 350°F (180°C).

2. Tip the hazelnuts, almonds and pistachios onto a large baking sheet and toast for 5 minutes. Add the sesame seeds to the pan and give it a shake, then toast for another 5–7 minutes until golden and fragrant.

3. Tip the coriander, fennel and cumin seeds onto a large separate baking sheet, and toast on the bottom rack of the oven for 2–3 minutes, shaking the pan halfway through. Take care as the spices can burn very quickly.

4. Grind the toasted coriander, fennel and cumin seeds using a spice grinder or mortar and pestle. Tip the toasted nuts into a small food processor and pulse until you have chunky crumbs, taking care not to over-process into a powder—you should have large pieces of nuts. If you prefer, you can just chop them with a knife.

5. Combine the seeds and nuts in a jar or airtight container and add the salt and Aleppo pepper, if using. Sprinkle over whatever you like. If stored in an airtight container, this will keep for many months.

Savory Seed Granola

Having condiments like this one can really lift simple meals. It is nut-free and bulked out with crunchy oats, making it slightly cheaper than the Dukkah opposite, but just as delicious. I sometimes add this to herby pestos and gremolatas for some added crunch and aromatic depth of flavor. It's great wherever you would add croutons, on a salad or as a final sprinkle on an open sandwich.

MAKES 20 SERVINGS
20 minutes

INGREDIENTS

½ TSP	Coriander seeds or ¼ tsp ground coriander
½ TSP	Cumin seeds or ¼ tsp ground cumin
½ TSP	Fennel seeds or ¼ tsp ground fennel
½ CUP (50 G)	Oats (gluten-free if needed)
¼ CUP (35 G)	Sunflower seeds
¼ CUP (35 G)	Pumpkin seeds
¼ CUP (35 G)	Sesame seeds
¼ TSP	Chile powder
¼ TSP	Chile flakes (optional)
½ TSP	Flaky sea salt
2 TBSP	Coconut oil

1. Toast the coriander, cumin and fennel seeds in a small dry frying pan over medium heat for about 2 minutes until fragrant. Transfer to a mortar and pestle and grind. If using ground spices, skip this step.

2. Tip the oats into a dry frying pan over medium heat and toast for 3–5 minutes, stirring occasionally.

3. Add the sunflower, pumpkin and sesame seeds to the pan and toast for another 5–8 minutes, stirring occasionally, until toasted and fragrant. Now add the fennel, cumin, coriander, chile and chile flakes (if using), along with the salt and coconut oil. Stir as the oil melts to combine it with the rest of the ingredients. Keep stirring for another couple of minutes.

4. Once the mixture is smelling toasted and aromatic and looks fairly dry, remove it from the pan and spread out on a tray to cool. It will harden as it cools.

5. Once cool, transfer to an airtight container or jar. It will keep for up to a month.

Aromatic Hot Agave

This is a Moroccan-inspired sweet and savory aromatic drizzle. It adds depth to marinades, balances vinaigrettes for salads, and is a perfect finishing touch on simple things like avocado toast or roasted corn.

MAKES 20 SERVINGS
20 minutes

INGREDIENTS

½ TSP	Nigella seeds
¼ TSP	Chile flakes (Aleppo pepper flakes work well too)
¼ TSP	Coriander seeds
¼ TSP	Cumin seeds
1 CUP (250 ML)	Agave or maple syrup
¼ TSP	Ground ginger
15	Twists of black pepper
⅛ TSP	Ground cinnamon
¼ TSP	Flaky sea salt
2	Strips of lemon rind

1. Lightly toast the nigella seeds, chile flakes, coriander seeds and cumin seeds in a dry frying pan over low heat for 3–5 minutes until fragrant.

2. Add the rest of the ingredients to the pan and stir together over low heat for 10 minutes. Allow to cool, then remove the lemon rind before pouring into a sterilized jar. If you like, you can strain to remove the aromatics at this point, but I quite like the crunchy texture.

3. This will keep for a month or more in the fridge.

GLUTEN-FREE   NUT-FREE   ALLIUM-FREE

Hot & Sweet Beet Tahini Sauce

This vibrant and versatile sauce is perfect for drizzling over roasted veggies, grains, or warm or cold salads. It's pretty punchy, so start with less chile and ginger and add more if you like. You could also use pre-cooked beets for this, but you'll get a slightly less intense color and flavor.

SERVES 10
2 hours

INGREDIENTS

3–4	Beets
⅓ OZ (10 G)	Red chile
1½ TBSP (20 G)	Fresh root ginger
⅓ CUP (100 G)	Tahini
2½ TBSP	Agave
½ TSP	Flaky sea salt
—	Juice of 3–4 limes or 3 lemons
—	Salt, freshly ground black pepper and olive oil

1. Preheat the oven to 400°F (200°C).

2. Wash the beets well and remove the tail and any stems and leaves (the stems are great pickled and the leaves are delicious sautéed with garlic).

3. Drizzle olive oil over the beets and season with salt and pepper. Rub the seasoning into each one, then wrap them individually and tightly in foil. Bake for 1½–2 hours or until they are very soft inside.

4. Remove from the oven and allow the beets to cool before unwrapping. Using gloves, rub the skins off each beet. They should come off fairly easily. If not, use a peeler.

5. Weigh out 10½ oz (300 g) of the beets and roughly chop. (Save the rest for another dish—they keep well in the fridge for 4–5 days.)

6. Roughly chop the chile and peel and chop the ginger. Add these to a high-speed blender, along with the beets, tahini, agave, salt and 2 tablespoons of olive oil. Add ⅔ cup (150 ml) water and blend until smooth. Add the juice of 3 limes, taste, and add more lime juice if you like. Taste and adjust the seasoning to your preference. Add more agave for sweetness or more water to thin it down.

7. The sauce will keep in a jar in the fridge for up to a week.

● GLUTEN-FREE ● NUT-FREE ● ALLIUM-FREE

How to Store Your Fresh Produce

Knowing how best to store your fresh produce will not only fight food waste but will also save you money. Here are my tips for keeping fruit and vegetables fresh for longer.

Vegetables

LEAFY GREENS (LETTUCE, SPINACH, KALE, ETC)

Remove any damaged leaves, then wash and dry thoroughly. Store them in a perforated plastic bag or airtight container lined with a paper towel. Place in the vegetable drawer of your refrigerator.

ROOT VEGETABLES (CARROTS, BEETS, ETC)

Remove the greens (if attached), as they can draw moisture from the roots. Store the roots in a perforated plastic bag or an open container with a damp paper towel to maintain moisture. Place in the vegetable drawer of your refrigerator.

BROCCOLI AND CAULIFLOWER

Place in a perforated plastic bag or wrap loosely in a damp paper towels and store in the vegetable drawer of your refrigerator. It's best to use these vegetables within a few days for optimal freshness.

ONIONS, SHALLOTS AND GARLIC

Store in a cool, dry and well-ventilated area. Keep them in a mesh bag or an open container to allow air circulation.

TOMATOES

Keep tomatoes at room temperature, away from direct sunlight. If they are not fully ripe, you can place them in a paper bag to accelerate the ripening process. Once ripe, use them within a few days.

POTATOES

Store potatoes in a cool, dark and dry place, ideally in a breathable bag or a cardboard box. Avoid storing them in the refrigerator, as the cold temperature can affect their texture and flavor.

PEPPERS

Store unwashed peppers in a plastic bag in the vegetable drawer of your refrigerator. Wash before using and ideally use them within a week.

CUCUMBERS

Keep cucumbers in the vegetable drawer of your refrigerator. If they are wrapped in plastic when purchased, keep them in the original packaging. Otherwise, you can store them in a perforated plastic bag.

GREEN BEANS AND PEAS

Keep these in a perforated plastic bag or an open container lined with a damp paper towels. Store them in the vegetable drawer of your refrigerator.

MUSHROOMS

Store mushrooms in a paper bag or a loosely closed container to allow for air circulation. Keep them in the refrigerator, preferably in the vegetable drawer. Only wash them if they are very dirty, otherwise brush the dirt off with a tissue or soft brush. If washing, avoid washing them until you are ready to use them.

ASPARAGUS

Trim the ends of the asparagus stalks and place them upright in a jar or container with about an inch of water. Cover the top loosely with a plastic bag and refrigerate.

CELERY

Wrap celery tightly in foil or place it in an airtight container to retain moisture. Store it in the refrigerator, preferably in the vegetable drawer.

BRUSSELS SPROUTS

Keep Brussels sprouts in a perforated plastic bag or an open container in the refrigerator's vegetable drawer. Remove any loose or discolored leaves before storing.

CORN

Leave the husks on and store corn in the refrigerator, preferably in the vegetable drawer. Use it as soon as possible for the best flavor, as the sugars in corn start converting to starch after harvest.

CHILES

Store unwashed chiles in a paper bag or a perforated plastic bag in the refrigerator's vegetable drawer.

BUTTERNUT SQUASH

Store in a cool, dry place with good air circulation. Avoid placing them directly on the floor, as this can cause rot. Once cut, wrap tightly in reusable wax wraps or place in a glass container and refrigerate.

ZUCCHINIS

These are best stored in a perforated plastic bag or an open container in the refrigerator's vegetable drawer.

CABBAGE

Remove any damaged outer leaves. If it came wrapped, keep it in the packaging or store it in a reusable plastic bag and don't cut it until you need to. Wrap any cut cabbage pieces tightly and store in the vegetable drawer of your refrigerator.

SCALLIONS

Place upright in a glass or jar with about an inch of water. Cover the top loosely with a plastic bag and store them in the refrigerator.

LEEKS

Trim off the dark green tops and store the leeks loosely wrapped in a damp paper towel in the vegetable drawer of your refrigerator. Alternatively, you can place them upright in a jar with about an inch of water.

RADISHES

Remove the greens and store radishes in a perforated plastic bag or an open container lined with a damp paper towel. Place them in the vegetable drawer of your refrigerator.

SWEET POTATOES

Store sweet potatoes in a cool, dry and dark place with good air circulation. Do not refrigerate them, as the cold temperature can alter their taste and texture.

EGGPLANTS

Store eggplants at room temperature, preferably in a cool and dry place. Avoid placing them in the refrigerator, as the cold can cause them to spoil faster.

Herbs

Remember to check your herbs regularly for any signs of wilting or decay. If you notice any damaged or yellowed leaves, remove them to maintain the freshness of the remaining herbs.

ROSEMARY, THYME AND OREGANO

Trim the ends of the stems and place the herbs in a glass or jar with about an inch of water. Cover the top loosely with a plastic bag and store them in the refrigerator. Alternatively, you can wrap them in a damp paper towel and place them in a perforated plastic bag before refrigerating.

MINT, CILANTRO AND PARSLEY

Treat these herbs like fresh flowers. Trim the ends of the stems and place them in a glass or jar with about an inch of water. Cover the top loosely with a plastic bag and refrigerate. Change the water every few days to maintain freshness.

BASIL

Trim the ends of the stems and place the basil in a glass or jar with about an inch of water. Cover the top loosely with a plastic bag and keep it at room temperature away from direct sunlight. Basil is sensitive to cold temperatures, so avoid refrigerating it.

DILL

Store dill in the refrigerator. You can either wrap the stems in a damp paper towel and place them in a plastic bag, or store the herb upright in a glass or jar with about an inch of water. Cover loosely with a plastic bag.

CHIVES

Trim the ends of the stems and place them in a glass or jar with about an inch of water. Cover the top loosely with a plastic bag and store them in the refrigerator. Chives can also be stored wrapped in a damp paper towel and placed in a plastic bag.

SAGE

Store sage in the refrigerator. Wrap the leaves loosely in a damp paper towel and place them in a plastic bag or an airtight container. Keep them in the vegetable drawer of your refrigerator.

TARRAGON

Store tarragon in the refrigerator. Wrap the stems in a damp paper towel and place in a plastic bag or an airtight container. Keep in the vegetable drawer of your refrigerator.

Fruit

APPLES

Store apples in a cool, dry place. Choose apples that are free from bruises or blemishes and separate any damaged ones to prevent spoilage from spreading. If storing for a longer period, wrap each apple in newspaper to help maintain their freshness.

PEARS

Pears should be stored at room temperature until they are ripe. Once ripe, you can refrigerate them to extend their shelf life. Check them regularly for ripeness by gently pressing near the stem end. They should yield slightly to pressure.

PLUMS

Plums can be stored at room temperature until they are ripe. Once ripe, they can be refrigerated to keep them fresh for a few more days. Like pears, check them regularly for ripeness by gently pressing near the stem end.

BERRIES (STRAWBERRIES, RASPBERRIES, BLACKBERRIES)

Berries are highly perishable and should be consumed as soon as possible. Store them unwashed in the refrigerator and avoid stacking them to prevent bruising. Rinse them just before consuming. Berries are best enjoyed within a few days of purchase.

CHERRIES

Cherries are best stored in the refrigerator. Place them in a ventilated container or leave them in the original packaging if it allows proper airflow. Only wash cherries right before eating to avoid moisture build-up, as excess moisture can lead to mold growth.

GRAPES

Grapes can be stored in the refrigerator. Place them in a ventilated container or leave them in the original packaging if it has proper airflow. Only wash the grapes right before eating to avoid moisture build-up.

BANANAS

Keep bananas at room temperature. If you want to slow down the ripening process, you can separate them from the bunch or wrap the stem ends with plastic wrap. If the bananas become overripe, you can peel and freeze them for later use in smoothies or baking.

ORANGES, GRAPEFRUITS AND CITRUS FRUITS

Citrus fruits can be stored at room temperature for a few days. For longer storage, place them in the refrigerator's crisper drawer or in a cool, well-ventilated place. Before storing, make sure they are dry to prevent mold growth.

Index

A

AGAVE SYRUP **10**
    AROMATIC HOT AGAVE **242**
    HOT & SWEET BEET TAHINI SAUCE **243**
ALMOND BUTTER
    MOCHA MESS **219**
    ULTIMATE VEGAN FRENCH TOAST **228**
ALMONDS
    CREAMY CELERIAC & ALMOND SOUP WITH PRESERVED LEMON GREMOLATA **148**
    FARINATA WITH ROMESCO, BROCCOLINI & EDAMAME **95**
    PEANUT BUTTER CHERRY JAM SEMIFREDDO **222**
AQUAFABA
    MOCHA MESS **219**
    SPICED CHILE CHOCOLATE MOUSSE **225**
ARTICHOKES
    ARTICHOKE, SPINACH & CHEESE PASTRY POCKETS **27**
    CRISPY ARTICHOKES WITH NORI MAYO **42**
    WHIPPED PEA, ARTICHOKE & ZA'ATAR WITH NEW POTATOES **101**
ASPARAGUS
    WHIPPED PEA, ARTICHOKE & ZA'ATAR WITH NEW POTATOES **101**

B

BALSAMIC TOMATO MACARONI WITH OLIVE PANGRATTATO **108**
BANANAS
    BANANA TAHINI ICE CREAM WITH PECAN CARAMEL CRUMBLES **221**
BASIL
    BUTTER BEANS WITH STICKY SOY PORTOBELLOS & THAI BASIL PESTO **120**
BEETS
    HOT & SWEET BEET TAHINI SAUCE **243**
    MISO QUINOA BEET BURGERS **23**
    MUSHROOM & ROOT VEGETABLE CENTERPIECE **170-2**
BOK CHOI
    GINGER & MISO NOODLE SOUP **150**
    HOT & STICKY STIR-FRY WITH RICE NOODLES **129**

BROCCOLI
    BROCCOLI PESTO PASTA **111**
    BROCCOLI STEMS & CHARRED BROCCOLI SNOW **30**
    FARINATA WITH ROMESCO, BROCCOLINI & EDAMAME **95**
    GREEN COCONUT NOODLE SOUP **146**
    HOT & STICKY STIR-FRY WITH RICE NOODLES **129**
    TANGY NEW POTATO SALAD **86**
BROWNIES
    FUDGY TAHINI BROWNIES **208**
BRUSSELS SPROUTS
    CRISPY KALE & BRUSSELS SPROUT SALAD **70**
BURGERS
    MISO QUINOA BEET BURGERS **23**
BUTTER BEANS
    AL LIMONE BUTTER BEAN PASTA **116**
    BUTTER BEANS WITH STICKY SOY PORTOBELLOS & THAI BASIL PESTO **120**
    GREENS & HERBS BUTTER BEAN PASTA **115**
    POINTED CABBAGE WITH SESAME WHIPPED BUTTER BEANS **82**
    SUN-DRIED TOMATO, CHILE & BASIL BUTTER BEAN PASTA **112**
BUTTERNUT SQUASH
    CRUSHED SPICED SQUASH WITH HAZELNUT GREMOLATA **72**
    ROASTED CHILE & SQUASH SPELT WITH SMOKY SUNFLOWER SEED CRUNCH **141-2**
    SPICED BAKED DAL WITH BUTTERNUT SQUASH **163**
    SPICED ROASTED SQUASH WITH POMEGRANATE MOLASSES & PISTACHIOS **187**

C

CABBAGE
    FRIDGE-RAID CRISPY PANCAKES **44**
    POINTED CABBAGE WITH SESAME WHIPPED BUTTER BEANS **82**
CAKES
    FILO CAKE WITH ORANGE & YOGURT (SOUFRA) **210-12**
    FUDGY TAHINI BROWNIES **208**

CALCIUM **14**
CANNELLINI BEANS
    CREAMY CELERIAC & ALMOND SOUP WITH PRESERVED LEMON GREMOLATA **148**
    LEEK & CANNELLINI BEAN GRATIN WITH OAT & HAZELNUT CRUMBS **168**
    LEMONY BEAN STEW **126**
CARAMEL
    BANANA TAHINI ICE CREAM WITH PECAN CARAMEL CRUMBLES **221**
    FUDGY TAHINI BROWNIES **208**
    VANILLA PUDDING WITH MISO CARAMEL **231**
CARROTS
    BLACK RICE WITH STICKY CARROTS & CITRUS **66**
    GRILLED LETTUCE WITH ORANGE SAUCE & SMOKY TOFU CRISP **80**
    LEMONY BEAN STEW **126**
    SMOKY PICKLED CARROT TART WITH EVERYTHING BAGEL SEASONING **194-5**
CASHEWS
    EGGPLANT & FREEKEH PIE **160**
    POINTED CABBAGE WITH SESAME WHIPPED BUTTER BEANS **82**
    LEEK & CANNELLINI BEAN GRATIN WITH OAT & HAZELNUT CRUMBS **168**
    PEANUT BUTTER CHERRY JAM SEMIFREDDO **222**
    ROASTED CASHEW BUTTER DRIZZLE **239**
    SMOKY PICKLED CARROT TART WITH EVERYTHING BAGEL SEASONING **194-5**
CAULIFLOWER
    CAULIFLOWER & POTATO QUINOA WRAPS WITH HARISSA YOGURT **97**
    CAULIFLOWER PIE WITH CRISPY QUINOA CRUST **165**
    CAULIFLOWER WITH HARISSA TAHINI & LENTILS **69**
    ROASTED CAULIFLOWER GNOCCHI **132**
CELERIAC (CELERY ROOT)
    CREAMY CELERIAC & ALMOND SOUP WITH PRESERVED LEMON GREMOLATA **148**
    MUSHROOM & ROOT VEGETABLE CENTERPIECE **170-2**
    SZECHUAN & PEANUT BUTTER SAUCY CELERIAC RIBBONS **65**

CHAI CUSTARD
    ROASTED PEARS WITH CHAI CUSTARD **214**
CHEESE, VEGAN
    ARTICHOKE, SPINACH & CHEESE PASTRY POCKETS **27**
    ONE-POT MUSHROOM LASAGNE **179**
CHERRIES
    SUMAC & POMEGRANATE CHERRIES ON BUCKWHEAT CRÊPES **226**
CHICKPEA FLOUR **10**
    CHICKPEA TOFU SALAD WITH GINGER-SOY DRESSING **38**
    PANISSE-STYLE CHICKPEA TOFU WITH HOT MAPLE SYRUP **37**
CHICKPEAS. SEE ALSO AQUAFABA
    BLACK RICE WITH STICKY CARROTS & CITRUS **66**
    CHICKPEA & BLISTERED TOMATO STEW **122**
    CRUSHED SPICED SQUASH WITH HAZELNUT GREMOLATA **72**
    MASALA-SPICED CHICKPEAS & COUSCOUS **74-6**
    MOCHA MESS **219**
    MUSABAHA WITH ZHOUG **51**
    SAUCY EGGPLANT, CHICKPEA & TOMATO BAKE **184**
    SPEEDY CHICKPEA & HARISSA SOUP **153**
    SPICED ROASTED SQUASH WITH POMEGRANATE MOLASSES & PISTACHIOS **187**
    SWEET POTATOES WITH TAHINI BUTTER CHICKPEAS **98**
    ZESTY CHICKPEA NORI WRAP **58**
CHILE OIL **10**
    HERBY SMACKED CUCUMBER SALAD WITH TAHINI & CHILE OIL **90**
CHILES
    HOT & STICKY STIR-FRY WITH RICE NOODLES **129**
    SUN-DRIED TOMATO, CHILE & BASIL BUTTER BEAN PASTA **112**
CHOCOLATE
    CHOCOLATE TART WITH SALTED OAT BASE **202**
    FUDGY TAHINI BROWNIES **208**
    MOCHA MESS **219**
    NO-BAKE FUDGY CHOCOLATE LOG (DOUKISSA) **204**
    SPICED CHILE CHOCOLATE MOUSSE **225**
    SUMAC & POMEGRANATE CHERRIES ON BUCKWHEAT CRÊPES **226**
COCONUT
    COCONUT CURRIED LENTIL DAL **118**
    STICKY COCONUT RICE WITH LIME & TOASTED COCONUT **188**
COCONUT CREAM
    CHOCOLATE TART WITH SALTED OAT BASE **202**
    MOCHA MESS **219**
COCONUT MILK
    BANANA TAHINI ICE CREAM WITH PECAN CARAMEL CRUMBLES **221**
    PEANUT BUTTER CHERRY JAM SEMIFREDDO **222**
COFFEE
    MOCHA MESS **219**
CONDIMENTS
    AROMATIC HOT AGAVE **242**
    DUKKAH **240**
    GREEK-STYLE VINAIGRETTE **236**
    HOT & SWEET BEET TAHINI SAUCE **243**
    LEMON & HERB SEED PARM SPRINKLE **238**
    PORCINI FURIKAKE **237**
    ROASTED CASHEW BUTTER DRIZZLE **239**
    SAVORY SEED GRANOLA **241**
COOKIES
    KALAMATA COOKIE ICE-CREAM SANDWICH **216**
CORN
    FRIDGE-RAID CRISPY PANCAKES **44**
    STIR-FRY BAKE WITH TOFU & PEANUT DRIZZLE **191**
COUSCOUS
    CRUSHED SPICED SQUASH WITH HAZELNUT GREMOLATA **72**
    HARISSA TOMATO COUSCOUS **102**
    MASALA-SPICED CHICKPEAS & COUSCOUS **74-6**
CREAM CHEESE, VEGAN
    CASHEW TOFU CREAM CHEESE **194-5**
    MUSHROOM & ROOT VEGETABLE CENTERPIECE **170-2**
    PULLED LEEKS WITH PISTACHIO CREAM **21**
CUCUMBER
    HERBY SMACKED CUCUMBER SALAD WITH TAHINI & CHILE OIL **90**
    MINCED TOFU WITH HERBY CUCUMBER SALAD & SRIRACHA MAYO **131**
CUSTARD
    ROASTED PEARS WITH CHAI CUSTARD **214**

D

DAL
    COCONUT CURRIED LENTIL DAL **118**
    SPICED BAKED DAL WITH BUTTERNUT SQUASH **163**
DATES
    BANANA TAHINI ICE CREAM WITH PECAN CARAMEL CRUMBLES **221**
    PEANUT BUTTER CHERRY JAM SEMIFREDDO **222**
    WARM DATES WITH PISTACHIOS & PRESERVED LEMON **24**
DIGESTIVE COOKIES
    NO-BAKE FUDGY CHOCOLATE LOG (DOUKISSA) **204**
DIPS
    GOCHUJANG DIPPING SAUCE **44**
    LEMONY SUNFLOWER SEED DIP **46**
    SMOKY ZUCCHINI DIP **56**
DRESSINGS
    CHICKPEA TOFU SALAD WITH GINGER-SOY DRESSING **38**
DUKKAH **240**
DUMPLINGS
    MUSHROOM DUMPLINGS **32-4**

E

EDAMAME BEANS
    FARINATA WITH ROMESCO, BROCCOLINI & EDAMAME **95**
EGGPLANTS
    EGGPLANT & FREEKEH PIE **160**
    MISO EGGPLANT ON HERBY RICE NOODLES **85**
    PULLED EGGPLANT RAGU WITH HUMMUS MASHED POTATO **139-40**
    SAUCY EGGPLANT, CHICKPEA & TOMATO BAKE **184**
    SLOW-ROASTED VEGGIE GNOCCHI **176**
ENVIRONMENTAL CONCERNS **15**
EVERYTHING BAGEL SEASONING
    SMOKY PICKLED CARROT TART WITH EVERYTHING BAGEL SEASONING **194-5**

F

FARINATA WITH ROMESCO, BROCCOLINI & EDAMAME **95**
FIBER **13**
FIG & GRANOLA FROZEN YOGURT POPS **206**
FILO PASTRY
    ARTICHOKE, SPINACH & CHEESE PASTRY POCKETS **27**
    EGGPLANT & FREEKEH PIE **160**
    FILO CAKE WITH ORANGE & YOGURT (SOUFRA) **210-12**
    SPANAKOPITA **173-4**
FLAXSEED **10**
FREEKEH
    EGGPLANT & FREEKEH PIE **160**
FRITTERS
    ZUCCHINI FRITTERS **40**

FRUIT, STORING **247**
FURIKAKE
    PORCINI FURIKAKE **237**

G

GARLIC BAKED ORZO WITH CRISPY KALE **166**
GINGER & MISO NOODLE SOUP **150**
GINGER-SOY DRESSING
    CHICKPEA TOFU SALAD WITH GINGER-SOY DRESSING **38**
GNOCCHI
    ROASTED CAULIFLOWER GNOCCHI **132**
    SLOW-ROASTED VEGGIE GNOCCHI **176**
GOCHUJANG DIPPING SAUCE **44**
GOMA DARE SAUCE **30**
GRANOLA
    FIG & GRANOLA FROZEN YOGURT POPS **206**
    SAVORY SEED GRANOLA **241**
GREEN BEANS
    BLISTERED GREEN BEANS WITH GINGER TOMATOES **28**
GREMOLATA
    CREAMY CELERIAC & ALMOND SOUP WITH PRESERVED LEMON GREMOLATA **148**
    CRUSHED SPICED SQUASH WITH HAZELNUT GREMOLATA **72**

H

HARISSA **10**
    CAULIFLOWER WITH HARISSA TAHINI & LENTILS **69**
    HARISSA TOMATO COUSCOUS **102**
    SPEEDY CHICKPEA & HARISSA SOUP **153**
HAZELNUTS
    CRUSHED SPICED SQUASH WITH HAZELNUT GREMOLATA **72**
    LEEK & CANNELLINI BEAN GRATIN WITH OAT & HAZELNUT CRUMBS **168**
HERBS
    GREENS & HERBS BUTTER BEAN PASTA **115**
    HERBY MARINATED OLIVES **53**
    HERBY SMACKED CUCUMBER SALAD WITH TAHINI & CHILE OIL **90**
    LEMON & HERB SEED PARM SPRINKLE **238**
    MINCED TOFU WITH HERBY CUCUMBER SALAD & SRIRACHA MAYO **131**
    MISO EGGPLANT ON HERBY RICE NOODLES **85**
    STORING **246**
HUMMUS
    PULLED EGGPLANT RAGU WITH HUMMUS MASHED POTATO **139–40**

I

ICE CREAM, VEGAN
    BANANA TAHINI ICE CREAM WITH PECAN CARAMEL CRUMBLES **221**
    KALAMATA COOKIE ICE-CREAM SANDWICH **216**
INGREDIENTS **10, 11**
    STORING FRESH PRODUCE **244–7**
IRON **13**

J

JAM
    LEEK & MISO ORZO WITH PRESERVED LEMON CHILE JAM **125**

K

KALAMATA COOKIE ICE-CREAM SANDWICH **216**
KALE
    CRISPY KALE & BRUSSELS SPROUT SALAD **70**
    GARLIC BAKED ORZO WITH CRISPY KALE **166**

L

LEEKS
    LEEK & CANNELLINI BEAN GRATIN WITH OAT & HAZELNUT CRUMBS **168**
    LEEK & MISO ORZO WITH PRESERVED LEMON CHILE JAM **125**
    PULLED LEEKS WITH PISTACHIO CREAM **21**
LEFTOVERS **11**
LEMONS
    AL LIMONE BUTTER BEAN PASTA **116**
    BLACK RICE WITH STICKY CARROTS & CITRUS **66**
    KALAMATA COOKIE ICE-CREAM SANDWICH **216**
    LEMONY BEAN STEW **126**
    LEMONY SUNFLOWER SEED DIP **46**
    ROASTED ZUCCHINIS WITH LEMONY WHIPPED TOFU **88**
LEMONS, PRESERVED
    CREAMY CELERIAC & ALMOND SOUP WITH PRESERVED LEMON GREMOLATA **148**
    LEEK & MISO ORZO WITH PRESERVED LEMON CHILE JAM **125**
    WARM DATES WITH PISTACHIOS & PRESERVED LEMON **24**
LENTILS
    CAULIFLOWER WITH HARISSA TAHINI & LENTILS **69**
    COCONUT CURRIED LENTIL DAL **118**
    MUSHROOM & ROOT VEGETABLE CENTERPIECE **170–2**
    ONE-POT MUSHROOM LASAGNE **179**
    SPICED BAKED DAL WITH BUTTERNUT SQUASH **163**
    SWEET POTATO SHEPHERD'S PIE **193**
LETTUCE
    GRILLED LETTUCE WITH ORANGE SAUCE & SMOKY TOFU CRISP **80**
LIMES
    BAKED MUSHROOM TACOS **181**
    SPICY MUSHROOM SKEWERS WITH PEANUT LIME SAUCE **77–8**
    STICKY COCONUT RICE WITH LIME & TOASTED COCONUT **188**

M

MANDARINS
    BLACK RICE WITH STICKY CARROTS & CITRUS **66**
MAPLE SYRUP **37**
MASALA-SPICED CHICKPEAS & COUSCOUS **74–6**
MAYONNAISE
    CRISPY ARTICHOKES WITH NORI MAYO **42**
    MINCED TOFU WITH HERBY CUCUMBER SALAD & SRIRACHA MAYO **131**
MERINGUES
    MOCHA MESS **219**
MISO **10**
    GINGER & MISO NOODLE SOUP **150**
    LEEK & MISO ORZO WITH PRESERVED LEMON CHILE JAM **125**
    MISO EGGPLANT ON HERBY RICE NOODLES **85**
    MISO QUINOA BEET BURGERS **23**
    ONE-POT MISO MUSHROOM PASTA BAKE **158**
    ROASTED CASHEW BUTTER DRIZZLE **239**
    VANILLA PUDDING WITH MISO CARAMEL **231**
MONEY-SAVING TIPS **11, 12**
MOUSSE
    SPICED CHILE CHOCOLATE MOUSSE **225**
MUSABAHA WITH ZHOUG **51**
MUSHROOMS
    BAKED MUSHROOM TACOS **181**
    BUTTER BEANS WITH STICKY SOY PORTOBELLOS & THAI BASIL PESTO **120**
    GINGER & MISO NOODLE SOUP **150**
    GREEN COCONUT NOODLE SOUP **146**
    MASALA-SPICED CHICKPEAS & COUSCOUS **74–6**
    MINI SESAME TOASTS **49**
    MUSHROOM & ROOT VEGETABLE CENTERPIECE **170–2**
    MUSHROOM DUMPLINGS **32–4**
    THE NEW CREAM OF MUSHROOM SOUP **144**
    ONE-POT MISO MUSHROOM PASTA BAKE **158**
    ONE-POT MUSHROOM LASAGNE **179**

OVEN-ROASTED MUSHROOM RISOTTO **183**
PULLED EGGPLANT RAGU WITH HUMMUS MASHED POTATO **139–40**
SAVORY OATS WITH SOY BUTTER SHIITAKE **134**
SPICY MUSHROOM SKEWERS WITH PEANUT LIME SAUCE **77–8**
SWEET POTATO SHEPHERD'S PIE **193**

N

NOODLES
    GINGER & MISO NOODLE SOUP **150**
    GREEN COCONUT NOODLE SOUP **146**
    HOT & STICKY STIR-FRY WITH RICE NOODLES **129**
    MISO EGGPLANT ON HERBY RICE NOODLES **85**
    STIR-FRY BAKE WITH TOFU & PEANUT DRIZZLE **191**
NORI
    CRISPY ARTICHOKES WITH NORI MAYO **42**
    MINI SESAME TOASTS **49**
    PORCINI FURIKAKE **237**
    ZESTY CHICKPEA NORI WRAP **58**
NUTRITION **12–15**
NUTRITIONAL YEAST **10**
    LEMON & HERB SEED PARM SPRINKLE **238**
NUTS. SEE ALSO INDIVIDUAL NUTS
    DUKKAH **240**

O

OATS
    CHOCOLATE TART WITH SALTED OAT BASE **202**
    LEEK & CANNELLINI BEAN GRATIN WITH OAT & HAZELNUT CRUMBS **168**
    PEANUT BUTTER CHERRY JAM SEMIFREDDO **222**
    SAVORY OATS WITH SOY BUTTER SHIITAKE **134**
OLIVES
    BALSAMIC TOMATO MACARONI WITH OLIVE PANGRATTATO **108**
    HERBY MARINATED OLIVES **53**
    KALAMATA COOKIE ICE-CREAM SANDWICH **216**
ONIONS
    CAULIFLOWER PIE WITH CRISPY QUINOA CRUST **165**
ORANGES
    FILO CAKE WITH ORANGE & YOGURT (SOUFRA) **210–12**
    GRILLED LETTUCE WITH ORANGE SAUCE & SMOKY TOFU CRISP **80**

P

PANCAKES
    FARINATA WITH ROMESCO, BROCCOLINI & EDAMAME **95**
    FRIDGE-RAID CRISPY PANCAKES **44**
    SUMAC & POMEGRANATE CHERRIES ON BUCKWHEAT CRÊPES **226**
PANGRATTATO
    BALSAMIC TOMATO MACARONI WITH OLIVE PANGRATTATO **108**
PANISSE-STYLE CHICKPEA TOFU WITH HOT MAPLE SYRUP **37**
PASTA
    AL LIMONE BUTTER BEAN PASTA **116**
    BALSAMIC TOMATO MACARONI WITH OLIVE PANGRATTATO **108**
    BROCCOLI PESTO PASTA **111**
    GARLIC BAKED ORZO WITH CRISPY KALE **166**
    GREENS & HERBS BUTTER BEAN PASTA **115**
    LEEK & MISO ORZO WITH PRESERVED LEMON CHILE JAM **125**
    ONE-POT MISO MUSHROOM PASTA BAKE **158**
    ONE-POT MUSHROOM LASAGNE **179**
    SUN-DRIED TOMATO, CHILE & BASIL BUTTER BEAN PASTA **112**
PEANUT BUTTER
    PEANUT BUTTER CHERRY JAM SEMIFREDDO **222**
    SAVORY OATS WITH SOY BUTTER SHIITAKE **134**
    STIR-FRY BAKE WITH TOFU & PEANUT DRIZZLE **191**
    SZECHUAN & PEANUT BUTTER SAUCY CELERIAC RIBBONS **65**
PEANUTS
    MISO EGGPLANT ON HERBY RICE NOODLES **85**
    SMASHED PEAS ON TOAST **54**
    SPICY MUSHROOM SKEWERS WITH PEANUT LIME SAUCE **77–8**
PEARS
    ROASTED PEARS WITH CHAI CUSTARD **214**
PEAS
    BAKED MUSHROOM TACOS **181**
    SMASHED PEAS ON TOAST **54**
    TOMATO & TOFU CURRY **136**
    WHIPPED PEA, ARTICHOKE & ZA'ATAR WITH NEW POTATOES **101**
PECANS
    BANANA TAHINI ICE CREAM WITH PECAN CARAMEL CRUMBLES **221**
PEPPERS
    FARINATA WITH ROMESCO, BROCCOLINI & EDAMAME **95**

SMASHED POTATOES WITH SPICY TOMATO SAUCE **92**
SPEEDY CHICKPEA & HARISSA SOUP **153**
PESTO
    BROCCOLI PESTO PASTA **111**
    BUTTER BEANS WITH STICKY SOY PORTOBELLOS & THAI BASIL PESTO **120**
PIES & TARTS
    CAULIFLOWER PIE WITH CRISPY QUINOA CRUST **165**
    CHOCOLATE TART WITH SALTED OAT BASE **202**
    EGGPLANT & FREEKEH PIE **160**
    SMOKY PICKLED CARROT TART WITH EVERYTHING BAGEL SEASONING **194–5**
    SPANAKOPITA **173–4**
PISTACHIOS
    MASALA-SPICED CHICKPEAS & COUSCOUS **74–6**
    PULLED LEEKS WITH PISTACHIO CREAM **21**
    SPICED ROASTED SQUASH WITH POMEGRANATE MOLASSES & PISTACHIOS **187**
    WARM DATES WITH PISTACHIOS & PRESERVED LEMON **24**
POMEGRANATE MOLASSES
    SPICED ROASTED SQUASH WITH POMEGRANATE MOLASSES & PISTACHIOS **187**
    SUMAC & POMEGRANATE CHERRIES ON BUCKWHEAT CRÊPES **226**
PORCINI FURIKAKE **237**
POTATOES
    CAULIFLOWER & POTATO QUINOA WRAPS WITH HARISSA YOGURT **97**
    PULLED EGGPLANT RAGU WITH HUMMUS MASHED POTATO **139–40**
    SMASHED POTATOES WITH SPICY TOMATO SAUCE **92**
    TANGY NEW POTATO SALAD **86**
    WHIPPED PEA, ARTICHOKE & ZA'ATAR WITH NEW POTATOES **101**
PROTEIN **12**

Q

QUINOA
    CAULIFLOWER & POTATO QUINOA WRAPS WITH HARISSA YOGURT **97**
    CAULIFLOWER PIE WITH CRISPY QUINOA CRUST **165**
    MISO QUINOA BEET BURGERS **23**

R

RASPBERRIES
    MOCHA MESS **219**
    ULTIMATE VEGAN FRENCH TOAST **228**

RICE
- BLACK RICE WITH STICKY CARROTS & CITRUS **66**
- LEMONY BEAN STEW **126**
- OVEN-ROASTED MUSHROOM RISOTTO **183**
- SPICY MUSHROOM SKEWERS WITH PEANUT LIME SAUCE **77-8**
- STICKY COCONUT RICE WITH LIME & TOASTED COCONUT **188**

S

SALADS
- CHICKPEA TOFU SALAD WITH GINGER-SOY DRESSING **38**
- CRISPY KALE & BRUSSELS SPROUT SALAD **70**
- HERBY SMACKED CUCUMBER SALAD WITH TAHINI & CHILE OIL **90**
- MINCED TOFU WITH HERBY CUCUMBER SALAD & SRIRACHA MAYO **131**
- TANGY NEW POTATO SALAD **86**

SEEDS
- AROMATIC HOT AGAVE **242**
- DUKKAH **240**
- LEMON & HERB SEED PARM SPRINKLE **238**
- SAVORY SEED GRANOLA **241**

SEMIFREDDO
- PEANUT BUTTER CHERRY JAM SEMIFREDDO **222**

SESAME SEEDS
- BROCCOLI STEMS & CHARRED BROCCOLI SNOW **30**
- MINI SESAME TOASTS **49**
- VANILLA PUDDING WITH MISO CARAMEL **231**

SHALLOTS
- PICKLED SHALLOTS **80**

SNOW PEAS
- STIR-FRY BAKE WITH TOFU & PEANUT DRIZZLE **191**

SOUP
- CREAMY CELERIAC & ALMOND SOUP WITH PRESERVED LEMON GREMOLATA **148**
- GINGER & MISO NOODLE SOUP **150**
- GREEN COCONUT NOODLE SOUP **146**
- THE NEW CREAM OF MUSHROOM SOUP **144**
- SPEEDY CHICKPEA & HARISSA SOUP **153**

SOY PRODUCTS **15**

SPANAKOPITA **173-4**

SPELT
- ROASTED CHILE & SQUASH SPELT WITH SMOKY SUNFLOWER SEED CRUNCH **141-2**

SPICES
- AROMATIC HOT AGAVE **242**
- BAKED MUSHROOM TACOS **181**

SPINACH
- ARTICHOKE, SPINACH & CHEESE PASTRY POCKETS **27**
- CAULIFLOWER & POTATO QUINOA WRAPS WITH HARISSA YOGURT **97**
- CHICKPEA & BLISTERED TOMATO STEW **122**
- GREENS & HERBS BUTTER BEAN PASTA **115**
- ONE-POT MISO MUSHROOM PASTA BAKE **158**
- SPANAKOPITA **173-4**
- SPEEDY CHICKPEA & HARISSA SOUP **153**
- SWEET POTATOES WITH TAHINI BUTTER CHICKPEAS **98**

STORING FRESH PRODUCE **244-7**

SUMAC & POMEGRANATE CHERRIES ON BUCKWHEAT CRÊPES **226**

SUNFLOWER SEEDS
- GREENS & HERBS BUTTER BEAN PASTA **115**
- LEMONY SUNFLOWER SEED DIP **46**
- ROASTED CHILE & SQUASH SPELT WITH SMOKY SUNFLOWER SEED CRUNCH **141-2**

SWEET POTATOES
- SWEET POTATO SHEPHERD'S PIE **193**
- SWEET POTATOES WITH TAHINI BUTTER CHICKPEAS **98**

T

TAHINI **10**
- BANANA TAHINI ICE CREAM WITH PECAN CARAMEL CRUMBLES **221**
- CAULIFLOWER WITH HARISSA TAHINI & LENTILS **69**
- FUDGY TAHINI BROWNIES **208**
- HERBY SMACKED CUCUMBER SALAD WITH TAHINI & CHILE OIL **90**
- HOT & SWEET BEET TAHINI SAUCE **243**
- MUSABAHA WITH ZHOUG **51**
- SMASHED PEAS ON TOAST **54**
- SWEET POTATOES WITH TAHINI BUTTER CHICKPEAS **98**

TARTS. SEE PIES & TARTS

TOAST
- MINI SESAME TOASTS **49**
- SMASHED PEAS ON TOAST **54**
- ULTIMATE VEGAN FRENCH TOAST **228**

TOFU **15**
- CHICKPEA TOFU SALAD WITH GINGER-SOY DRESSING **38**
- GINGER & MISO NOODLE SOUP **150**
- GRILLED LETTUCE WITH ORANGE SAUCE & SMOKY TOFU CRISP **80**
- HOT & STICKY STIR-FRY WITH RICE NOODLES **129**
- MINCED TOFU WITH HERBY CUCUMBER SALAD & SRIRACHA MAYO **131**
- MINI SESAME TOASTS **49**
- MUSHROOM DUMPLINGS **32-4**
- THE NEW CREAM OF MUSHROOM SOUP **144**
- PANISSE-STYLE CHICKPEA TOFU WITH HOT MAPLE SYRUP **37**
- ROASTED ZUCCHINIS WITH LEMONY WHIPPED TOFU **88**
- SMOKY PICKLED CARROT TART WITH EVERYTHING BAGEL SEASONING **194-5**
- SPANAKOPITA **173-4**
- STIR-FRY BAKE WITH TOFU & PEANUT DRIZZLE **191**
- TOMATO & TOFU CURRY **136**
- ULTIMATE VEGAN FRENCH TOAST **228**
- VANILLA PUDDING WITH MISO CARAMEL **231**

TOMATOES
- BALSAMIC TOMATO MACARONI WITH OLIVE PANGRATTATO **108**
- BLISTERED GREEN BEANS WITH GINGER TOMATOES **28**
- CHICKPEA & BLISTERED TOMATO STEW **122**
- EGGPLANT & FREEKEH PIE **160**
- HARISSA TOMATO COUSCOUS **102**
- ONE-POT MUSHROOM LASAGNE **179**
- PULLED EGGPLANT RAGU WITH HUMMUS MASHED POTATO **139-40**
- SAUCY EGGPLANT, CHICKPEA & TOMATO BAKE **184**
- SLOW-ROASTED VEGGIE GNOCCHI **176**
- SMASHED POTATOES WITH SPICY TOMATO SAUCE **92**
- SPEEDY CHICKPEA & HARISSA SOUP **153**
- SPICED BAKED DAL WITH BUTTERNUT SQUASH **163**
- SUN-DRIED TOMATO, CHILE & BASIL BUTTER BEAN PASTA **112**
- SWEET POTATO SHEPHERD'S PIE **193**
- TOMATO & TOFU CURRY **136**

TORTILLAS
- BAKED MUSHROOM TACOS **181**

V

VANILLA PUDDING WITH MISO CARAMEL **231**

VEGAN DIET **12-15**

VEGETABLES
- FRIDGE-RAID CRISPY PANCAKES **44**
- MUSHROOM & ROOT VEGETABLE CENTERPIECE **170-2**
- STORING **244-5**

VINAIGRETTE
- GREEK-STYLE VINAIGRETTE **236**

VITAMIN B12 **14**

W

WALNUTS
- NO-BAKE FUDGY CHOCOLATE LOG (DOUKISSA) **205**
- PULLED EGGPLANT RAGU WITH HUMMUS MASHED POTATO **139-40**
- SWEET POTATO SHEPHERD'S PIE **193**
- TANGY NEW POTATO SALAD **86**

WRAPS
- CAULIFLOWER & POTATO QUINOA WRAPS WITH HARISSA YOGURT **97**
- ZESTY CHICKPEA NORI WRAP **58**

Y

YOGURT, VEGAN
- CAULIFLOWER & POTATO QUINOA WRAPS WITH HARISSA YOGURT **97**
- FIG & GRANOLA FROZEN YOGURT POPS **206**
- FILO CAKE WITH ORANGE & YOGURT (SOUFRA) **210-12**
- LEMONY SUNFLOWER SEED DIP **46**
- MASALA-SPICED CHICKPEAS & COUSCOUS **74-6**
- MINTY YOGURT **40**

Z

ZA'ATAR
- WHIPPED PEA, ARTICHOKE & ZA'ATAR WITH NEW POTATOES **101**

ZHOUG
- MUSABAHA WITH ZHOUG **51**

ZUCCHINIS
- BAKED MUSHROOM TACOS **181**
- ROASTED ZUCCHINIS WITH LEMONY WHIPPED TOFU **88**
- SAUCY EGGPLANT, CHICKPEA & TOMATO BAKE **184**
- SLOW-ROASTED VEGGIE GNOCCHI **176**
- SMOKY ZUCCHINI DIP **56**
- ZUCCHINI FRITTERS **40**

Acknowledgments

This book is dedicated to my mom, who cooked for 4 kids plus one big kid (my dad) with so much love, every single day when we were growing up, and still puts a heroic effort into her dinner parties and Sunday lunches. She taught me that the kitchen table is the center of the universe, where we bond with family and friends and show our love for them through food. This book is for you, Mom, to sit among the endless cookbooks in your collection.

I want to say a huge thank you to the brilliant team that worked on this book: Joe Woodhouse, whose vision was so aligned with mine, that shooting the photographs was not only a breeze but so much fun too. Kitty Coles, who helped me style the first section of the shoot and helped me choose the props—Kitty, you are absolutely brilliant at your job, have such beautiful energy and gave me so much confidence to continue the food styling without you. Rosie Mackean and Lucy Turnbull who both stepped in for Kitty and did the most incredible job. And a big thank you to the styling assistants Clare Cole, Kristine Jakobsson and Fernanda Milanezi.

Of course a huge thank you to Emily Brickell, who guided me at every step and the wider team at Ebury for making this book happen.

I also want to thank all of the lovely group of people who tested every single recipe in the book—it meant the world to me to receive all of your honest and incredibly helpful feedback.

Last but not least, I want to thank Ben Lebus who gave me my first role in recipe writing, always guided and pushed me to be better and who opened up so many doors for me.

Conversion Tables

Oven Temperatures

°C	FAN °C	°F	GAS MARK
140°C	120°C	285°F	GAS MARK 1
150°C	130°C	300°F	GAS MARK 2
160°C	140°C	325°F	GAS MARK 3
180°C	160°C	350°F	GAS MARK 4
190°C	170°C	375°F	GAS MARK 5
200°C	180°C	400°F	GAS MARK 6
220°C	200°C	425°F	GAS MARK 7
230°C	210°C	450°F	GAS MARK 8
240°C	220°C	475°F	GAS MARK 9

Weights

METRIC	IMPERIAL
15 G	½ OZ
25 G	1 OZ
40 G	1½ OZ
60 G	2 OZ
75 G	2½ OZ
100 G	3½ OZ
150 G	5½ OZ
175 G	6 OZ
200 G	7 OZ
225 G	8 OZ
250 G	9 OZ
275 G	10 OZ
350 G	12 OZ
375 G	13 OZ
400 G	14 OZ
425 G	15 OZ
450 G	1 LB

Volume

METRIC	IMPERIAL
30 ML	1 FL OZ (2 TBSP)
60 ML	2 FL OZ (¼ CUP)
80 ML	3 FL OZ (⅓ CUP)
150 ML	5 FL OZ (⅔ CUP)
300 ML	10 FL OZ (1¼ CUPS)
450 ML	15 FL OZ (2 CUPS)
600 ML	20 FL OZ (2½ CUPS)
700 ML	24 FL OZ (3 CUPS)
950 ML	1 QUART (4 CUPS)
1 LITER	34 FL OZ (4¼ CUPS)
1.2 LITERS	40 FL OZ (5 CUPS)
1.25 LITERS	42 FL OZ (5¼ CUPS)
1.5 LITERS	50 FL OZ (6⅓ CUPS)
1.6 LITERS	54 FL OZ (6¾ CUPS)
1.75 LITERS	60 FL OZ (7⅓ CUPS)
1.8 LITERS	61 FL OZ (7½ CUPS)
2 LITERS	68 FL OZ (8½ CUPS)

Measurements

METRIC	IMPERIAL
0.5 CM	¼ INCH
1 CM	½ INCH
2.5 CM	1 INCH
5 CM	2 INCHES
7.5 CM	3 INCHES
10 CM	4 INCHES
15 CM	6 INCHES
18 CM	7 INCHES
20 CM	8 INCHES
23 CM	9 INCHES
25 CM	10 INCHES
30 CM	12 INCHES

Please note that these recipes have been tested using metric measurements, and imperial conversions may yield slightly different results. Either way, follow one set of measurements only—never mix metric and imperial.

First published in 2025 by
Interlink Books
An imprint of Interlink Publishing Group, Inc.
46 Crosby Street
Northampton, Massachusetts 01060
www.interlinkbooks.com

Published simultaneously in the United Kingdom by Ebury Press, an imprint of Ebury Publishing, part of the Penguin Random House group of companies.

Copyright © Christina Soteriou 2025
Photography except pages 9, 26, 29, 96, 113, 207 © Joe Woodhouse 2025
Photography on pages 26, 29, 96, 113, 207 © Nassima Rothacker 2025
Photography on page 9 © Nathan Wolf Grace 2025

All rights reserved. No part of this publication may be reproduced, stored in a retrieval system or transmitted in any form or by any means, electronic, mechanical, photocopying, recording, or otherwise, without the prior written permission of the publisher. No part of this book may be used or reproduced in any manner for the purpose of training artificial intelligence technologies or systems.

Library of Congress Cataloging-in-Publication Data available
ISBN 978-1-62371-623-3

Design by Imagist
Photography by Joe Woodhouse
Food styling by Christina Soteriou
Prop styling by Kitty Coles

Color origination by Altaimage Ltd, London
Printed and bound in in China by C&C Offset Printing Co., Ltd

We have done our best to ensure the information in this book is correct, however it is advised to always check food labels when cooking for anyone with allergies, as manufacturing processes and transparency varies between brands and food producers. Always consult with the person for whom you are catering on their specific allergies and foods to avoid. The author and publishers disclaim, as far as the law allows, any liability arising directly or indirectly from the use, or misuse, of the information contained in this book.